GROWING MORAL

GUIDES TO THE GOOD LIFE

Stephen Grimm, series editor

GROWING MORAL
A Confucian Guide to Life

Stephen C. Angle

OXFORD
UNIVERSITY PRESS

Oxford University Press is a department of the University of Oxford. It furthers
the University's objective of excellence in research, scholarship, and education
by publishing worldwide. Oxford is a registered trade mark of Oxford University
Press in the UK and certain other countries.

Published in the United States of America by Oxford University Press
198 Madison Avenue, New York, NY 10016, United States of America.

© Oxford University Press 2022

CIP data is on file at the Library of Congress
ISBN 978-0-19-006289-7

DOI: 10.1093/oso/9780190062897.001.0001

9 8 7 6 5 4 3 2 1

Printed by LSC communications, United States of America

Dedicated in loving memory to
Charles Edwin Angle III
(1939–2015)

TABLE OF CONTENTS

SERIES EDITOR'S FOREWORD

Several ancient philosophers held that the point of studying ethics was not just to learn about ethics—as one might learn about chemistry, astronomy, or history—but to become a better human being. They also recognized that this was not easy to do. In order for thinking about ethics to make a difference in our lives, they argued that our habits and inclinations needed to be educated right alongside our minds. They therefore claimed that what mattered to living well was not just what we thought but *how* we thought, and not just how we thought but how we emotionally responded to the world and to other people.

The books in this series highlight some of the transformative ideas that philosophers have had about these topics—about the good life, and the practices and ways of life that help us to pursue it. They tell us what various philosophers and traditions have taken to be most important in life, and what they have taken to be less important. They offer philosophical guidance about how to approach broad questions, such as how to structure our days, how to train our attention, and how to die with dignity. They also offer guidance about how to deal with the sort of everyday questions that are often neglected by scholars, but that make up the texture of our lives, such as how to deal with relationships gone wrong, family disruptions, unexpected success, persistent anxiety, and an environment at risk.

Because the books are written by philosophers, they draw attention to the reasons and arguments that underlie these various claims—the particular visions of the world and of human nature that are at the root of these stances. The claims made in these books can therefore be contested, argued with, and found to be more or less plausible. While some answers will clearly compete with one another, other views will likely appear complementary. Thus a Confucian might well find that a particular practice or insight of, say, Nietzsche's helps to shed light on his or her way of living in the world, and vice versa. On the whole, the idea is that these great philosophers and traditions all have something to teach us about how to be more fully human, and more fully happy.

Above all, the series is dedicated to the idea that philosophy can be more than just an academic discipline—that it can be, as it was for hundreds of years in the ancient world, a way of life. The hope is also that philosophy can enhance the ways of life we already feel pulled toward, and help us to engage with them more authentically and fully.

Stephen R. Grimm
Professor of Philosophy
Fordham University
September 2019

ACKNOWLEDGMENTS

How and why to live one's life as a Confucian have occupied me for years, and I have many friends, colleagues, and family members to thank for their guidance and support along the way. One theme of this book is that Confucianism is relevant today in all corners of the world, but it remains the case that I have learned a great deal from the efforts of colleagues in China to think through and revitalize Confucian practice; my thanks to Peng Guoxiang, Chen Ming, Tang Wenming, Fang Zhaohui, and Gan Chunsong, in particular. Some of my initial thinking about this book took place while I was on a Berggruen Fellowship in Beijing in 2016–2017; I appreciate the great support there from Song Bin and all her colleagues.

Over the last decade or so I have become increasingly invested in the idea that philosophy is meant to be lived, not just thought about; and that approaching philosophy as a way of life means that we philosophers should teach differently (as well as live differently). A conversation with Amy Olberding about her own teaching was a breakthrough for me; Steven Horst, Tushar Irani, Lori Gruen, and Elise Springer at Wesleyan have all helped me as well, and, in some cases, this has led to shared experimentation with new forms of teaching. I treasure my experience co-directing an NEH Summer Institute in 2018 on "Reviving Philosophy as a

Way of Life" with Meghan Sullivan and Stephen Grimm; many thanks to them and to all the wonderful participants, as well as to Elizabeth Moemeka and Gaby Parke for making things flow so smoothly. More generally, thanks to all who make Wesleyan such a healthy place for open-minded scholarship and experimental pedagogy—with special appreciation to my colleagues in the Fries Center for Global Studies with whom it has been a pleasure to work over these last three years.

I have done my best to write a book that is not weighed down by scholarly rigor, but nonetheless builds on the best scholarship on Confucianism. I appreciate the feedback from colleagues and students at presentations I gave at Boston University, Fordham University, Yale-NUS College, Peking University, Duke Kunshan University, and Skidmore College. I also want to acknowledge the fine work of many previous translators of the classic texts I quote here; I take responsibility for all translations but have consulted others' work and sometimes follow them quite closely.

I have bounced ideas and drafts off a number of friends and colleagues, all of whom have my deepest gratitude for helping me to think more deeply and write more clearly. Many thanks to Bin Song and Justin Tiwald, in particular, as well as to Michael Roth and Stephanie Weiner. Several members of the "GodTalk" group in Middletown read a draft manuscript and offered terrific feedback; thanks especially to Janet Brooks. My mother and stepfather both read the entire manuscript and provided invaluable feedback. I have also been thrilled at the support and care that Lucy Randall, Hannah Doyle, and their colleagues at OUP, in addition to series editor Stephen Grimm, have lavished on this project. I've never had an editor contribute so much to making a book better.

As you'll soon see, rituals are important parts of Confucian living. Rituals are meant to be heartfelt, not just going through the motions; indeed, one of the measures of one's moral growth is the degree to which this is true. One of the nicest academic rituals is closing a book's acknowledgments by thanking one's family: they, after all, are the ones without whom the book would have been impossible. And at least in this case, I find it easy to live up to the ritual. My father passed away before the book got going, but I hope that his joy in life continues to animate these pages. The love and wisdom of my mother and stepfather, stepmother, parents-in-law, brothers, sisters-in-law, their families, aunts and uncles and cousins, and the friends who might as well be family—all of them give my life meaning and richness. My wife is my life partner and best friend, and for both of us our greatest joy is our daughters. They are both college graduates now, launching their own lives and careers, but the COVID-19 pandemic has meant that they each have spent months living back at home. One side benefit of this precious time together has been learning from their perspectives on many of the issues I address in the book. To Sam and Rachel and all my family, my love and gratitude.

A NOTE ON ABBREVIATIONS

Passages from classical Confucian texts that are available in multiple translations are cited by text and chapter or passage number, rather than by specific edition. For recommendations about which editions to consult, please see Further Reading. I use the following abbreviations:

LY = *Lunyu* (or *Analects*); citations include book and passage number

MC = *Mengzi* (or *Mencius*); citations include book and passage number

XZ = *Xunzi*; citations include chapter and line number from Hutton's translation

Part One

What Is Confucianism?

INTRODUCTION

"He drew his last breath" had never been more than an antiquated figure of speech to me, but that changed on June 1, 2015. My brother and I sat by our father's side, his bony, fragile hands in ours, as he drew his last breath. It was faint, a struggle. The broad outlines of what happened in the next hours and days will be familiar to many readers and easily imagined by the rest: hugs and tears, moments for reflection, laughter mixed with more tears, a service in a church, a graveside service. Some details are more particular, such as the Congregationalist church or the sailor playing "Taps," as befits a retired member of the navy. And then there was the quiet voice in my head—an occupational hazard of philosophers, perhaps—asking "Why?" I wasn't questioning what we were doing, all of which felt right, but I could not help thinking about why these emotions and rituals seemed both apt and important. Why is it significant that we honor and mourn a parent who dies? Does it matter how we do so—and again, why?

Confucianism tells us that going through mourning rituals is a crucial part of living a good life. Kongzi (also known as Confucius, after whom Confucianism is named; 551–479 BCE) is the most famous of the 2500-year-long tradition's philosophers; later we will meet a few others. Even though Kongzi lived more than two millennia ago and on the other side of the earth from some of this book's readers, Confucianism's teachings about how to live continue to resonate everywhere there are parents, children, and families; everywhere people feel stirrings of compassion for others, but sometimes selfishly ignore them; everywhere people wonder about how to interact with their environment. In some cases, such as my father's funeral, Confucians can help us make sense of what we are already doing; in others, they encourage us to live our lives differently and better. The Confucian tradition has undergone many changes as it has evolved over the centuries, and that process continues down to the present. At the heart of the tradition, though, are profound insights into the human condition that have much to teach us today.

* * *

Or so I say . . . but I understand that for many, this may initially sound like a hard sell. Few outside of East Asia are familiar with Confucianism, and in fact there aren't many self-identified Confucians in the world today. South Korea probably has the most, yet according to surveys, only a small percentage of Koreans chose "Confucian" from among the list of religious affiliations.[1] Can Confucianism really have a role in our lives today?

The Korean government survey presented Confucianism as a religion. This immediately leads to a problem, though, because many people (including many contemporary Koreans) think of "religion" as an all-or-nothing matter of identity and belief, whereas Confucianism is not centered around belief in a deity. I happen to agree with modern scholars of religion that "religion" should be understood in a broader, more inclusive way, and that Confucianism is numbered among the world's religions. But to avoid confusion, in this book I'll talk of Confucianism as a kind of philosophy instead. Philosophy is reasoned reflection on the biggest questions about our lives and our world. From its earliest origins in various civilizations, philosophy has been intimately connected with the question of how to live—and thus with issues we confront every day. Historically and still today, many philosophers have not just been thinkers but also teachers or life coaches or advisors: people who can help us as we seek to understand how we should live. And implicit in a philosopher's offering of reasons for how to live is a recognition that you may consider other reasons, other philosophies. Philosophies are not all-or-nothing and, partly for this reason, philosophical traditions change over time as they adapt to new realities and adopt new ideas.

At its core, Confucianism describes a way for humans to live together in our world: a way characterized at its best by joy, beauty, and harmony. Confucian writings explain what it is about our psychologies and our environment that makes the Confucian way of life so natural and successful. Confucian teachers of course lived in particular times, places, and cultural contexts; Kongzi himself lived most of his life in the small state of Lu, which roughly corresponds to the present-day province of Shandong in eastern China. But Kongzi and his many later followers were not writing just for the people of Lu, nor even just for the people of China (a concept that did not exist in Kongzi's day). They believed that following their way of life enabled people to live the best possible lives—lives that were cultured and fully human.

People today know that there are many different values and ways of life embraced by others around the globe. We have unprecedented access to information, many of us live in highly pluralistic societies, and we are all too aware of the radical, sometimes violent insistence of some people on their way of life above all others. Amidst all this diversity, any claim that Confucians offer the uniquely best insights into how we humans should live may seem implausible. From a contemporary vantage point, though, each of us can appreciate and learn from the Confucians' inquiries into how to live and adopt as much of a Confucian way of life as makes sense to us. We can consider it alongside other traditions if we wish or take it on as our guiding philosophy of life. Or we can also simply seek to learn about it, in an attempt to understand more deeply a historically important way of thinking about the good life, among other ways of thinking that will be explored in this book series.

In short, this book is putting Confucianism forward as a philosophy of life for your consideration. It is for everyone who has questions—even just a vague sense of dissatisfaction—about how their lives are going presently, especially concerning the wide range of issues that the Confucians address explicitly. And it is worth taking seriously because . . . well, one reason is that I say so! Other than my mother (Hi Mom!), few readers will know me, but I have studied Confucianism for more than three decades and taught it for almost as long; both my students and I can speak to its helpful guidance on many occasions, from mundane conflicts with roommates to larger questions like how to balance commitments to family, work, and community involvement. Another reason is that for more than two millennia, many millions of people— mostly in East Asia—learned from its insights about their lives and their societies.

As soon as I say this, though, alarm bells may start to sound. It is common for modern people, even those who grew up in East Asia, to share some negative stereotypes about the Confucian-influenced values of pre-modern Asia. Am I proposing that people today should model themselves on inflexible, authoritarian patriarchs? Submissive women with bound feet? Or that we should put saving face above telling the truth and sacrifice individuality for the collective? It probably goes without saying that these stereotypes are uncharitable caricatures, but I also must acknowledge that, as with many stereotypes, they contain elements of truth. Traditional Confucians emphasized the authority of elders—even though this authority could be challenged—and in many contexts, they expected men to have the dominant roles. Foot-binding was not an explicitly Confucian practice, but Confucians did little to criticize it. Acting with propriety was always emphasized, even if (as we will see) sincerity was also prized. And there are some ways in which traditional Confucians did, indeed, downplay personal uniqueness, at least when compared to many modern cultures.

There are two critical things to keep in mind as we proceed. First, there are differences between the ways that Confucians believe we should act and the contemporary values of most modern societies. This is a good thing: if there were no differences, then there would be no possibility of learning anything! Of course, the mere existence of a difference does not automatically mean that there is anything much to learn; I doubt that we should send aspiring chefs to study with cannibals. But many differences do open up possibilities for learning, as this book's chapters will demonstrate.

Second, like all living traditions, Confucianism has grown and changed over the centuries as new ideas and new social realities presented themselves. I'll save the historical details for the next chapter; suffice it to say for now that Confucian thinkers have been able to recognize when changed conditions call for changed viewpoints, even while stressing the importance of connection to the past. This self-critical development has continued into the twentieth and twenty-first centuries, a period of particular challenge for Confucians. Dramatic social and political changes throughout the Confucian heartlands in East Asia have led to the rethinking of some key values. This book is itself part of an ongoing conversation about the meaning of Confucianism, because its goal is not to describe how Confucians lived centuries ago, but rather to suggest how to live as a Confucian today. For example, I am convinced that Confucianism must jettison certain patriarchal assumptions that would otherwise serve as obstacles to the full ethical development of women. The reasons for this development lie within Confucianism itself, as I will explain later on; rejecting patriarchy is a form of Confucian self-criticism, not an imposition on the tradition from outside. The Confucianism for which this book is a kind of advertisement, in short, is both conservative and progressive. It conserves the insights and values that have always formed the core of the tradition, while simultaneously adapting some teachings to incorporate new findings or to resolve old tensions.

* * *

We'll soon get a chance to meet the five Confucian philosophers who are the book's main heroes; for each of them, personal moral growth and broader social harmony are mutually supporting goals. The core of the book comes in Part Two, "How To Be A Confucian." Each of its eight chapters is designed around a recommendation central to the Confucian vision of living a good life: "Be Filial", "Follow Rituals", "Read in the Right Way", "Pay Attention", and so on. The chapters contain modern-day examples and advice, even though they are grounded in the tradition's values and reasoning. Part Three then looks at the ways in which we can grow as moral beings. What is it to make a commitment to living well? What is the role of forced, conscious self-control, and why do Confucians think that spontaneity is preferable to control? How do we overcome selfishness, and is it realistic to aspire to be a "sage," as the Confucians claim? Time and again, we will see that ancient teachings mesh with modern experiences and even with modern science.

Part Four turns to some of the challenges facing modern Confucians. What should we make of the many hierarchies—between young and old, men and women, rulers and subjects—embraced by traditional Confucians? Can Confucianism flourish in a culturally diverse modern society? In each case, the progressive style of Confucianism I adopt here has ready answers. I recognize, though, that even while some non-Western ideas and values have been quite influential globally in the last century, Confucianism has not. The book's final chapter explores the reasons for this and argues that the Confucian way of life discussed here can have a bright future.

For Confucianism to flourish again, people like you need to discover its relevance to topics that matter, from personal growth and education to cultural and social issues. The point of embracing a philosophy of life, after all, is to live in a way that feels right and makes sense. Part of this is reflective and intellectual: reading, thinking, talking with others. That is where this book fits in. But an equally important part is practical: learning to live your life according to the values you choose. Does Confucianism help you to discover more joy, meaning, and harmony in your life? Try it and see.

2 | THE HISTORY OF CONFUCIANISM

On a January day almost five hundred years ago, traveling home from his latest service to the empire, Wang Yangming succumbed to a lingering illness. He was fifty-six years old. We are separated from Wang by half a millennium in time and (at least for many readers) vast distance in space, not to mention differences of culture, technology, and so on. And among the five main heroes of this book, Wang's distance from us in time is by far the least. Even so, a key premise of this book is that the Confucian tradition in which Wang played a vital role still can speak to us today. Partly this is because the tradition has continued to evolve: just as Wang's Confucianism built on but also critiqued aspects of his predecessors' Confucianisms, and theirs did the same to their predecessors' Confucianisms, so too does modern Confucianism both build on and critique what has come before. The tradition also speaks to us today because the lives these great Confucians lived and the insights they had are still appealing and meaningful. Let's now meet the five men who anchor the book.

Yes, I did just say "five men." Why only men? I believe that Confucian ideas are not inherently sexist, but Confucianism has spent its entire life embedded in highly patriarchal societies. The nature of these East Asian patriarchies differed from other varieties around the world, but the fact remains that women's roles were constrained, and Confucian men did little to criticize this. I do not mean to imply that there were no Confucian women. Many women found the values and practices of the Confucian tradition appealing, and a few elite women were able to publish treatises on its philosophy. Their topic was almost invariably the education of women, understood as playing their own, limited roles in society. In contrast, male Confucian thinkers typically took their subject to be humanity and our place in the cosmos. There is plenty of specific teaching about different roles, but the core ideas and values are quite general. Following the lead of many modern Confucians, I'll therefore take Confucianism to apply equally to all, and use gender-neutral language to express this. Later, I'll revise the traditional Confucian approach to gender, but my basis for doing so will be Confucian ideas themselves, including those of the most radical of the female Confucian thinkers. Except on issues related to gender, I think you'll find this book's five heroes to be pretty good guides.

Without further ado, then, the principal sources for this book's ideas are:

- Kongzi (or Confucius), 551–479 BCE, pronounced kong-dz
- Mengzi (or Mencius), 4th c. BCE, pronounced meng-dz
- Xunzi, 3rd c. BCE, pronounced hsün-dz
- Zhu Xi, 1130–1200 CE, pronounced jew-hsee
- Wang Yangming, 1472–1529 CE, pronounced wahng yahng-ming

A few clarifications about these names might be in order before we get to the individuals themselves. In East Asia, it's customary to give one's family name first, in keeping with the general principle of moving from more encompassing to more specific. (Even today, Chinese postal addresses give the country first, followed by the province, city, street, and so on, ending with the recipient's name.) So, for the two people on the list who are widely known by their names, the family name is first: Zhu Xi is Mr. Zhu; Wang Yangming is Mr. Wang.[1] The names I have listed for our other three heroes also encompass their family names, but there are additional wrinkles. First, the additional "zi" at the end of the name means "Master," and they are usually referred to today in the honorific way that their students would address them: as Master Kong (Kongzi), Master Meng (Mengzi), and Master Xun (Xunzi). Second, when Jesuit missionaries showed up in China in the sixteenth century, they invented Latinized names for the two most famous Confucians: Kongzi became "Confucius" and Mengzi became "Mencius." I'll eschew these Latinized names when referring to the philosophers themselves, mainly to avoid any suggestion that Kongzi and Mengzi are somehow qualitatively different from the later folks, but I will use the term "Confucianism" to refer to the tradition as a whole. As will become clear, the tradition is not just the property of Kongzi; he plays an important role, but so do the teachers and thinkers who follow him.[2]

Emphasizing these five philosophers as representative of the Confucian tradition is not terribly controversial. If you asked scholars to list the Most Influential Confucians of All Time, these five would be at the top of everyone's lists. Admittedly, some of these five are traditionally thought of as rivals—and perhaps even as holding incompatible views. Xunzi criticized Mengzi for having a naïve view of human nature; Wang Yangming criticized Zhu Xi for a rigid and insufficiently experience-based philosophy. On top of that, the "Classical" thinkers (the first three) are generally thought to have pretty different ideas on key subjects than the later "Neo-Confucians" (Zhu and Wang). All true. But what I am doing is ultimately the same kind of thing that each of the post-Kongzi thinkers did, in his own way: synthesizing the best ideas within this on-going tradition, sometimes a bit creatively, in keeping with the core commitments of the tradition (on which I think all of my heroes would agree). In my dialogue with other contemporary developers of Confucianism, I seek to show how the insights of Kongzi and his inheritors continue to resonate.

* * *

China in 551 BCE, when Kongzi is born, is a society on the precipice of massive change. The Zhou family have been the official "kings" of China since their ancestors founded the Zhou dynasty half a millennium earlier, but lately the Zhou king has lacked real power. The feudal lord of each region is actually in charge, with overall peace kept relatively successfully by agreement among the lords. Underlying social and technological changes are underway, though, that spell the doom of this system. Agriculture is getting more efficient, populations are growing, warfare is increasing in scale and destructiveness, and nobles and commoners alike are becoming more ambitious. Within a century or so, China will enter the "Warring States" era as the feudal lords—now calling themselves "kings"—use new ideas (and massive armies) to vie with one another. The Warring States era comes to a close in 221 BCE with the founding of a new dynasty headed by China's first "emperor"; the Classical era has ended and the Imperial era begun.

But I am getting ahead of myself. Returning to Kongzi, we must keep in mind that as mentioned earlier, Confucianism is not based on divine revelation. Kongzi is not a prophet. He is a committed (though often frustrated) follower of those he feels to be the legitimate leaders of his homeland, and he is a scrupulous student of the culture and history of his people. Indeed, in the most reliable source of his ideas, the *Analects*, he is recorded as having said, "I transmit rather than invent."[3] Kongzi values traditions and rituals, for reasons that we will explore throughout this book. Still, he is being modest when he says that he merely transmits. His teaching, his theorizing, and his personal example all express the crucial idea that one's worth comes from one's personal development and virtue, not from one's birth. He has transformed the category of "*junzi*," which literally meant the son of a lord, to mean a morally "exemplary person" from any social background. Aristocrats, he has discovered, all too often failed to be *junzi*, and in his travels he is regularly willing to harangue the powerful men he encounters. His many students came from all walks of life and are instrumental in spreading his understanding of China's traditions. Kongzi doesn't invent "Confucianism," exactly, but he puts his imprint firmly on it.

Before moving on to Mengzi, let me say a few words about our main sources for the ideas of Kongzi and his followers. If you look back to the previous paragraph, you'll see that I wrote that Kongzi "is recorded as having said" the thing about transmitting rather than innovating. I'm being cautious because we really don't know for sure if he wrote this or even if he said it. Scholars have been debating for centuries what the exact origin of the different chapters in the *Analects* might be. Some think that Kongzi, like Socrates in ancient Greece, did not write anything himself. Instead, and again like Socrates, it seems likely that much or all of the *Analects* was written by students, perhaps closely based on things they remembered the Master saying and perhaps not. There is reason to believe that some of the *Analects* may even have been written many decades after Kongzi's death, thus expressing ideas of an evolving Confucian school. Something similar is probably true of the texts collecting the ideas of our other two Classical-era heroes, the *Mengzi* and the *Xunzi*. Because this book aims to synthesize Confucian ideas over a long time span rather than to present the specific ideas of one individual or text, these issues won't impact us too deeply; but it is good to keep in mind what is actually lying behind the translated words you'll see in these pages.

Mengzi and Xunzi lived well after Kongzi, in the heart of the Warring States era. We know relatively little for sure about their early lives, though there are several famous stories about Mengzi's mother's dedication to raising him well. For example, when the young Mengzi (long before he actually had earned the "zi" for "Master" in that title) announced that school learning was boring and useless, she is said to have turned to the loom on which she had been weaving and cut the cloth in half. Half-finished cloth was worthless—just like a half-finished education. Mengzi was a dedicated student thereafter. He was older than Xunzi, probably dying before the end of the 4th century BCE. Xunzi's life spanned the 4th and 3rd centuries BCE. But the two had broadly similar careers: travelling from one state to another seeking to persuade rulers to follow the Confucian Way; sometimes finding political office but never great political success; and teaching many students how to be good people and, in so doing, how to lead their societies well. Both thinkers left behind texts bearing their names. The *Mengzi* text is—like the *Analects*—composed of dialogues, while the *Xunzi* is a collection of topical essays. As a result, we get a better sense of Mengzi's personality than Xunzi's. For example, Mengzi's boldness comes through when he suggests to King Hui of Liang that he is failing in his responsibility as the "people's parent" because while there is fat meat in the king's kitchen, people outside the palace are starving.[4] Both thinkers make frequent references to the exemplary life and teachings of Kongzi and seek to develop Kongzi's approach to life, which is why we can think of them all as "Confucians." Living perhaps half a century later than Mengzi, Xunzi is clearly aware of Mengzi and is sometimes quite critical of what he sees as Mengzi's naïveté; but as we'll see, the differences between the two do not run as deep as has often been thought.

Around the end of Xunzi's life, the Warring States period ends when the King of Qin successfully unifies China under his rule, declaring himself the "first emperor" and founding the Qin Dynasty. The draconian (and deeply anti-Confucian) policies that enabled his conquest are initially effective at creating unity out of the many contending peoples and cultures of early China. A single writing system, system of measurement, currency, and so on help to initiate China's Imperial era. Such an all-encompassing and rigid unification ultimately proves fragile, however, and soon after the Qin founder's death, his dynasty collapses, replaced by new rulers who temper Qin ideas of unity with more inclusiveness and flexibility. The resulting Han dynasty, which lasts for four centuries, will ultimately make Confucianism into a kind of state ideology. The *Analects* is revered as a Classic text, alongside others like the *Book of Changes* and the *Book of Odes*. Confucian scholars staff imperial educational institutions. The result is "Imperial Confucianism": state-sponsored, widely followed, but less lively than the Classical Confucianism that had come before. For many centuries, Confucian ideas are (for the most part) lived superficially and studied scholastically.

In the meantime, Buddhism is flourishing. Buddhism begins in India around the same time that Kongzi lived, and by the early first millennium CE it has reached China. It grows in China and reaches Korea and Japan as well during the millennium of Imperial Confucianism. Throughout this time, Buddhist and Confucian insights cross-pollinate, which initially leads to new forms of Buddhism and eventually results in a major new development within Confucianism: the revival of creative Confucian thinking that we label "Neo-Confucianism." Neo-Confucians critique the scholastic, ossified forms of Confucianism that had come to dominate Chinese culture and education, arguing that Confucianism is meant to be a personal teaching, shaping how each person lives—and ultimately, calling on each person to strive toward sagehood. Neo-Confucians insist that important classical texts (especially *Mengzi*) have been neglected or misunderstood. Neo-Confucianism starts as a small, radical movement that is periodically proscribed by those in power, but by the 12th century CE, it is increasingly dominant intellectually. The person at the center of this movement is Zhu Xi.

Zhu Xi (1130–1200 CE) lived in south-eastern China, and while he held various local governmental offices over his career, tensions with powerful court figures as well as his own interests in teaching and scholarship kept him away from the capital. He gathered, organized, and published the writings of path-breaking Neo-Confucians from the prior century; he developed his own creative synthesis of their ideas; he taught many students, often in private academies that he ran; and he wrote brilliant new commentaries on many classical-era works. Taken together, Zhu's efforts form the core of Neo-Confucianism. A little more than a century after his death, Zhu's interpretation of Confucianism was mandated as authoritative in the state educational system, which meant that for six hundred years, every educated person in China studied his ideas.

Becoming established orthodoxy is a two-edged sword: on the one hand, it means that many will study your philosophy, but on the other hand it means that often they will do so without really engaging with the ideas, seeking only to do well on the exams. As we will see in a later chapter, this was something that concerned Zhu himself, long before he was declared orthodox. But it still meant that for Neo-Confucianism to remain a vital, developing school of thought, people had to find ways to challenge the orthodoxy. The most important such revisionist is Wang Yangming (1472–1529). Unlike Zhu Xi, Wang had a glorious public career, serving both as a minister in the Ming dynasty royal court and as a successful general. Like Zhu, he saw Confucian teachings as deeply relevant to the way one lived one's life, and like Zhu he taught many students over the years. His collected conversations with these students, as well as his philosophical correspondence, were edited and then published by some students—which, ironically, he had discouraged! Where Zhu believed that reading and scholarship were central to developing as a Confucian, Wang put more emphasis on personal introspection; Wang worried that scholarship often led to wooden repetition of past slogans, rather than to immediate responses to the unique challenges before one. As we will see, though, in many ways Wang's teachings align with those of Zhu and their classical forebearers.

In the centuries after Wang Yangming, Neo-Confucianism gradually declined in creativity and influence even while Confucian practices remained ubiquitous throughout China. The 20th century, in particular, was a bad century for Confucianism. In 1905, a last-ditch effort to reform a floundering empire led to the abandonment of the civil-service exam system, around which higher education in China had been based for centuries. This was followed, in 1911, with the collapse of the last dynasty itself. In 1915, Chinese intellectuals inaugurated a "New Culture Movement" that sought fundamental changes to Chinese values, practices, and even the Chinese language under the slogan of "wholesale Westernization." Educational institutions remade themselves around Western disciplines like "philosophy" and "religion," and activists criticized traditional family structures and arranged marriages. In many ways this was a more pervasive "cultural revolution" than the later Maoist movement of that name. Some Confucians dug in their heels and defended the old ways; others sought to adapt and argue for Confucianism as one "philosophy" among others. Confucianism did not die, but after the first decades of the 20th century, it would need to find new ways to be relevant in the modern world.

The story of what happens next for Confucianism is still being written. On the one hand, some political leaders have tried to manipulate it as a shallow ideology of loyalty to power. On the other hand, an increasingly international group of thinkers have sought to update Confucianism or synthesize it with other traditions of thought (from Marxism to liberalism and beyond). I will say more about these efforts in this book's concluding chapter. For now, it is time to turn to the core question that has animated Confucians throughout the centuries: How should we live our lives?

Part Two

How to Be a Confucian

3 | BE FILIAL

If we judge by the Ten Commandments, "Honor your father and your mother" is the fifth-most important thing to the God of the Book of Exodus. Honoring your parents is significant—it comes before the prohibitions on murder and adultery—but not as important as the primacy of God, which is covered in the first four commandments. Arguably, parents are even less important in early Christianity: "And call no one your father on earth, for you have one Father—the one in heaven."[1]

For Confucians, in contrast, your relationship with your parents is the most important thing. Your parents' caring for you was critical to your growing into the person you are today, and Confucians have consistently asserted that a child's attitude toward his or her parents is the vital "root" from which goodness will grow.[2] The proper attitude to have toward your parents, Confucians teach, is filial piety. I will say more about what filial piety means in a moment, but first let's note another contrast with the Judeo-Christian tradition. Judeo-Christian moral teachings come from outside the self: they come from

God and are largely independent of whatever experiences you have had (even if some Jews or Christians argue that they have had experiences of God). Confucian teachings aim to build on, shape, and cultivate what you already are. By the time people encounter a Confucian text or teacher, they are already living lives, experiencing feelings, in the midst of relationships. Chief among these relationships is that between parent and child. Confucians believe that what we should become is based on what we already are. Our best selves must grow from our earlier and more basic selves, and so we start with parent–child (or caregiver–child) relations and with families.

Let us begin with a statement by Kongzi that can easily lead us astray if we do not consider it carefully. In response to a question about filial piety, Kongzi is recorded as saying "Never disobey."[3] Is that it, then? Filial piety just means obedience? Before jumping to that conclusion, let's note a few more things. First, the same passage in the *Analects* continues by recounting a follow-up conversation. Later in the day, Kongzi tells someone else about the "Never disobey" comment, and this student asks Kongzi what he meant. In other words, he was skeptical that Kongzi could really think that filial piety was just about obedience. And indeed, Kongzi clarifies, saying: "When they are alive, serve them with propriety; when they are dead, bury them with propriety, and sacrifice to them with propriety." This is both more and less than simple obedience: more, because an attitude of "propriety" is demanded throughout one's parents' lives and even after they have passed away; less, because Kongzi leaves room for the possibility that one might be able to disobey with propriety.

In another passage, Kongzi elaborates on this latter possibility:

The master said, "In serving your father and mother, remonstrate gently. If you see that they are committed to not following your lead, be respectful without disobedience and energetic without resentment."[4]

Gentle remonstration is the very essence of disobeying with propriety; one seeks to invert the usual relationship and become one's parent's teacher. At least in this passage, the room for such resistance is distinctly limited, but we'll be coming back to the question of how one should relate to problematic parents and other caregivers.

For now, let us focus on a different question: is one's behavior or one's attitude more central to filial piety? Consider the following two passages from the *Analects*:

Zi You asked about filial piety. The Master said, "Nowadays filial piety is merely what one might call providing nourishment. But even dogs and horses can receive nourishment. If you are not respectful, where is the difference?"[5]

Zi Xia asked about filial piety. The Master said, "The demeanor is difficult. If there is work, the younger bear the toil of it; if there are wine and food, the elder get the best portions. Did only this ever count as filial piety?"[6]

Speaking with two different students, Kongzi makes essentially the same point. Yes, there are specific kinds of behavior that go along with filial piety—the young toiling on behalf of the elderly, the elderly getting the best nourishment—but this is insufficient to count as filial piety. (Kongzi considers his "nowadays" to be a pale imitation of the era of ancient sages.) What really matters is how one feels as one performs these actions, which Kongzi expects will be manifest in one's demeanor. It is not just that one feeds one's parents, but that one does so with respect. In yet another passage, he stresses the anxiety that it is appropriate to feel as one's parents age. To be sure, this does lead to specific behavior ("While your father and mother are alive, do not travel far; if you do travel, have a definite destination"[7]), but ultimately it is the underlying attitude that is most important. We'll soon see that the attitude is so important because it is the foundation for one's broader moral growth.

Before moving on, there are two more things to note about what filial piety is. First, according to most Confucians, it has a natural basis. Mengzi is explicit about this: "Among babes in arms there are none that do not know how to love their parents."[8] Recent scholars of Confucianism have emphasized how consistent this is with modern theories of evolutionary psychology, according to which "kin preference is part of our nature and cannot be ignored."[9] The second point is the converse of the first: because filial piety is cultivated out of natural roots, it is not an obligation that is imposed on us. As a contemporary scholar puts it, rather than thinking of filial piety as something that one "owes" to one's parents in return for their giving one existence, it is "the sense of gratitude, reverence, and love that children naturally feel when they are nurtured, supported, and cared for by people who do so out of a loving concern for the child's well being."[10]

To sum up so far, filial piety is an attitude of love and respect for one's parents, feelings that are natural to have (at least to a degree, and at least partly in response to loving concern from one's parents), and filial piety is expressed both through characteristic actions and in one's demeanor. As this summary suggests, we need to know more about how one cultivates the initial feelings into full-blown filial piety, as well as address what happens when one's parents fail to nurture one with loving care. This also brings us to two other issues. First, can a combination of love and respect really be one, unified attitude? Immanuel Kant famously argued that these two feelings are importantly different from one another, with love associated with closeness while respect is associated with distance.[11] I think Kant is partly right about this, but we do not need to see the two feelings as opposed. Instead, we can draw on the central Confucian idea of harmony and recognize that filial piety is in fact a complex attitude in which love and respect are balanced with one another. This is already implicit in Kongzi's remarks about providing nourishment with respect and about "gentle remonstrance," in which one's love tempers the way one expresses one's judgment (which is tied to the idea of respect). Indeed, I expect that striving for the most fruitful balance between respect and love for one's parents is a common experience. A good method of cultivating filial piety should help us to achieve such a balance.

The second issue is to see that filial piety is not an attitude that one just happens to have some of the time, but is (or at any rate, should be) a more pervasive aspect of one's character. The goal is not to act in a filial fashion only when it is easy, nor is it to feel filial piety only now and again. The goal is to become a person characterized by filial piety, to be a filial daughter or son. This means thinking of filial piety not just as an attitude but also as a virtue. Virtues are positive traits of character. One who has a given virtue will reliably react to situations with the attitudes, demeanors, and actions associated with that virtue. Crucially, Confucians recognize that while many virtues have their origins in our natural reactions, the attainment of a given virtue takes time and is a matter of degree. That is, one can be fairly filial or quite filial or very filial—or even be a paragon of filial piety, perhaps meriting the title of "sage." In short, when we ask how to become filial, we are not just asking what a filial person does, but also exploring how to develop ourselves from whatever degree of filial piety we currently have to become a more pervasively filial person.

* * *

I have been explaining what Confucians believe filial piety to be. If you already identify as a Confucian, you might already have a good reason to try to become more filial. The point of this book, though, is not only to spell out what it is to be a Confucian today, but also to propose to all readers that Confucian ideas and practices are valuable and worth a try. So, why should you want to be a more filial person?

It is important to be clear on the kind of question under consideration here. When I ask, "Why should you want to be a more filial person," I am addressing people who have (or have had) a parent or parents, or in some cases caregivers who have filled a parental role; and who have experienced at least some filial piety (if the Confucians are right and its beginnings are natural). So, the question is not addressed to beings with no experience of a parent–child relationship who would need to have the whole enterprise of filial piety explained and justified from the ground up. We humans do not typically ask ourselves whether we should really love our parents, and rightly so! The question of whether filial piety should be more or less central in our lives, though, is a live question that is well worth asking. We can each take steps toward making ourselves—and our friends, relatives, or children—more or less filial, and deciding whether to do so requires more than just the intuitive sense that one should love one's parents. It requires philosophical reflection.

So, why is filial piety important, and why should we strive to be more filial? The answer given in the *Analects* is that filial piety is the "root" of humaneness. Humaneness here means the height of human virtuosity. If one devotes oneself to cultivating filial piety, multi-faceted virtuosity will grow, and with it an increasingly humane world. We will have ample opportunities in later chapters to flesh out what these ideals of virtuosity and humaneness encompass. For now, take it for granted that they are attractive and practical: what is presently at stake is understanding why filial piety is so central to their realization.

There are a few reasons why filial piety is critical. First and most obviously, it is the starting point for one's moral growth. One's earliest relationships are with one's parents or parent-like caregivers. As P. J. Ivanhoe has insightfully recognized, in one's relationships with parents one first experiences love and care being prioritized over power and interest.[12] More generally, it is within one's family that one first has opportunities to interact with others, and thus to gradually learn how it feels to interact well—to fit in with others, to both learn from and eventually to teach others. As other scholars have put it, our ability to successfully inhabit the many roles we take on in society "originates in and radiates from concrete family feelings."[13] It's important to add that nothing in this analysis depends on a child's being biologically related to their parent or parents. The caring is what matters; when that is absent, as in tragic cases of children long-abandoned in orphanages, normal moral growth can be much more difficult.[14]

Second, more than just a starting point, filial piety is actually a microcosm of the broader and deeper virtuosity that is our ultimate goal. We have already seen that filial piety is a complex state that requires one to learn how to balance love and respect. This is a skill one can get better at, as one learns to pay attention to what's important in which context, and this type of skill applies to all virtues. Similarly, one has to learn how to apply rules. In many American households, it is a rule that children should not begin eating at a family meal until everyone is served and their parents are seated. Perhaps there is also some further ritual, like saying grace. It is not easy to wait; my twenty-two-year-old daughter sometimes still forgets. But over time, one internalizes the point of a rule like this—expressing respect and gratitude—and becomes more fluid both at following it and at realizing when it's not necessary to follow it. Ultimately, being a virtuous person means being responsive to particular details of context rather than rigidly following rules, and all of this complexity is already bound up in filial piety.

The third reason for filial piety's centrality is that it remains significant throughout one's life, even if the details vary as both one's parents and oneself pass through various stages of the life cycle. One's own filial piety serves as a model to one's children, just as reflecting back on one's relationship with parents informs and motivates one's own caring for children. For all these reasons, it is understandable that Confucians see filial piety as of the first importance.

However, what if one's own parents are not so exemplary? Given how common it is for humans to err in small ways and large, it should be no surprise that many Confucians have considered precisely this question. We have already taken note of Kongzi's discussion of "remonstrance"; Xunzi puts the point even more strongly, saying that the "greatest conduct" consists in following "righteousness and not one's father."[15] The majority of Confucian reflections on bad parents, though, lean in the other direction. In a famous anecdote in the *Analects*, Kongzi praises a son who hid from the authorities the fact that his father stole a sheep.[16] The *Mengzi* recounts several stories about the ancient sage Shun, who was known as a paragon of filial piety. In one, Shun's father tries to kill him so that Shun's stepbrother can take the throne; Shun's only response is to deftly avoid the threat and continue to show love for his parents.[17] Extreme cases like this lead Ivanhoe to argue that traditional Confucianism demands too much. He argues that the stories about Shun overplay the value of a "grin and bear it" attitude; instead, children of bad parents should be able to decide whether to cultivate and show their parents "at least some degree of filial piety."[18]

Shun's case is not only extreme but also rare, and we should be cautious about what lessons to draw that relate to more likely scenarios in our own lives. After all, Confucians do not insist that we follow inflexible rules, come what may. Confucians do not demand that one do what one cannot do. As we will see in later chapters, Confucians call upon each of us continually to strive to be better, but the way we should act at a given moment in time depends only on what we are capable of at that moment. Shun's forbearance borders on the super-human. Any normal person would have cracked under the pressures the *Mengzi* describes and left home, putting distance between oneself and such a troubled family, and quite possibly turned in the would-be-murderer to the police. Keep in mind, though, that such a step can be taken from a place of love and respect: perhaps such dramatic steps offer the only plausible path toward a better future for one's father.

More generally, Confucians will counsel us always to do our best to respond to challenges within our families out of the feelings of love and respect that lie at the core of filial piety.[19] And they will quickly remind us that all too often, a key reason that one's parent's behavior looks problematic actually lies in one's own selfishness. Confucians hold that selfishness is the deep source of problems in our world. Consider the case of a son, the eldest in his family, who in his youth was gregarious but also troubled, and over time grew to resent his shy younger sister for the way she seemed to receive most of their mother's attention. One day the grown son learns that his mother, without consulting him, has made certain arrangements that favor the sister (who has been struggling) over himself (now financially secure). Enraged, he vows never to speak to his mother (or sister) again. Let us grant that the mother acted badly here, in the actions that precipitated the crisis and perhaps even in showing favoritism when her children were younger. But in allowing his anger and resentment to narrow his vision, the son is unable to see all the harm he is causing.

As this case shows, learning to live a good life is not just about responding to parental love with love and respect of one's own. We must cultivate filial piety, which should broaden into other virtues, and we must work to reduce selfishness. Importantly, Confucians do not just tell us we need to do these things, but also provide specific directives that we can put into practice. One of the main categories of these practical teachings is "ritual."

4 | FOLLOW RITUALS

Have you ever learned that a friend's parent was desperately ill and been unsure what to say? Some will be comfortable with "I am so sorry; I will pray for her," but what if you do not pray? Perhaps you say those words anyway, or else substitute something like "I will keep her in my thoughts." In my own experience, merely resolving to "think" about someone when she is nearing death seems like too little—too little both to my friend and to his dying mother—but to spell out every detail of my reaction seems like too much. My empathy for him and his family, my hopes that her last hours will be peaceful and pain-free, my worries about what this might mean for him and his siblings, my re-kindled feelings and reflections from my own father's passing: this is all too complex, personal, and inchoate to be easily expressed. Instead of being tongue-tied, maybe "I will keep her in my thoughts" isn't so bad after all.

The Confucians' term for the plethora of semi-scripted practices that shape our social world is *li*, which I translate as "ritual." Another possible translation would be "etiquette";

certainly, the table manners, thank-you notes, and so on that one might associate with etiquette are included within the scope of *li*. But *li* is both broader and weightier than modern notions of etiquette. *Li* ranges from religious or public ceremonies all the way to smaller-scale interactions like the example with which I began. Part of the point of *li* is that all these behaviors, even the most seemingly trivial, have an importance in producing good people living in good societies; by rendering *li* as "ritual" I am endeavoring to emphasize its importance. To many readers, the idea of "ritual" will probably sound rather alien: it is not something that we think about very often today, save perhaps for anthropologists studying the "rituals" of distant cultures. Another point of using the word "ritual," then, is precisely to foreground the fact that this is something that modern people tend to neglect or forget. Our world is shot through with ritual, but we downplay or ignore it. To live as Confucians recommend, we need to recognize and embrace the centrality of ritual in our lives.

I have just been saying that I use the translation "ritual" in order to call attention to the significance of *li*, but don't we sometimes refer to behaviors as "mere rituals," emphasizing not their significance but their emptiness? True enough—and ironically, this is another advantage of thinking of *li* as ritual. When *li* are done well they are invested with emotional meaning, but to learn them sometimes we do need to just "go through the motions," and in occasional cases this might even be apt for adults. After all, even when one is going through the motions, one is taking part in the external behaviors that make up the ritual, and this can have positive effects. Consider the ritual common in many contemporary societies to wear dark colors and speak in muted tones at a funeral. In a straight-forward way this helps to make it possible for any of the participants to enter into a mood of somber reflection, even if some of them have no desire to do so. An adolescent at the funeral of a great-uncle she barely knew may be feeling more bored than reflective, but by forcing herself not to crack jokes with her cousins, she follows the external script of the ritual—and so we can say that she is "disciplined" by the ritual.

Boredom is not the only enemy of ritual discipline; often enough, we find ourselves sorely tempted to tell others "what we really think of them." Amy Olberding has written incisively (and hilariously) about the joys and sense of release that can come with rudeness.[1] But Olberding and other scholars of Confucianism have also emphasized the values that can result when we allow ourselves to be disciplined through ritual: the work of being polite is often worth it. As Sor-hoon Tan has observed, "Polite and non-confrontational postures, facilitated by ritual acts understood by all, even in situations of a serious conflict of interests, are . . . powerful means of increasing the chances of an outcome acceptable to all."[2] Even in heated debates, members of the US Congress refer to one another in formal, somewhat stilted ways: they address comments to "the member from South Carolina" or "the gentlewoman from New York." Of course, these and other rituals do not guarantee a harmonious result, but by encouraging an atmosphere in which one can attend to the others' statements, the possibility of constructive conversation is increased. In addition, beyond any value that may result from ritualized interactions, part of the point of rituals is that they provide us with an accessible communicative shorthand. Rather than struggling to express one's complex and perhaps conflicted feelings, one says "my thoughts are with you" or "fine, and you?" or "Congratulations!" So while sometimes it takes work to be polite, in another sense rituals make things easy for us.

Perhaps you will say they make things too easy. If all I have to do is mouth some words to count as fulfilling a ritual, how can this have the significance that the Confucians assign it? The answer lies in a second dimension of ritualized behavior: not just what one does, but also how one does it. Even if they are a kind of shorthand, rituals can still be done well or badly. Olberding's writings are again an excellent source of insight, especially her analysis of the role that "style" plays. To adapt one of her examples, imagine yourself waiting in line at a coffeeshop. Even surrounded by strangers, one can be gracious, friendly, and patient, perhaps exchanging a wry smile at others' foibles with a neighbor in line. On the other hand, what if in front of you an elderly patron pays for his coffee by laboriously writing a check, and you huff with impatience and roll your eyes, shifting weight from foot to foot while conspicuously checking your watch? Think of what that expresses to others—whether or not the elderly person sees you.[3] Such manifest impatience or even misanthropy goes a long way toward undermining the point of the ritual of waiting in line, which isn't simply efficiency but includes an expression of equal respect. Confucians therefore use the word *li* in two different ways: to refer to the rituals we live out, and to refer to the propriety with which we live them.

Propriety is a skill one can develop over time; the more one does so, the more we can say that one has the virtue of propriety. When we enact a ritual, we are doing more than just disciplining our current selves (by, for example, restraining impatience or boredom and trying to look friendly); we are also engaging in a process that can change us over time. Confucians describe this process in many (not always entirely compatible) ways which we'll explore later. The core idea is simple, though: by restraining and channeling our behavior, rituals help us to notice things that we might not pay attention to otherwise. Over time, we get better at noticing, and as we do so we start to respond to situations more fluidly, with less self-imposed discipline.

* * *

At least to some degree, this chapter's Confucian advice to follow rituals is fairly easy to implement. We do regularly follow rituals, even if many of us had not been aware that this is what we are doing, and even if we all should put more effort into consistently following rituals than we do. But especially once the idea of "ritual" has been made more explicit, a number of questions arise. For example, should one always follow the rituals or are there times when it's better to make an exception? "Ritual" also seems very old-fashioned; do they ever change? Can we invent new ones? Finally, it can often seem that rituals reinforce existing hierarchies: only people of "good breeding" know which fork to use at an elaborate dinner, and so on. Is this also true of the rituals that Confucians think are important? Should we be concerned that rituals fit poorly with modern egalitarian values?

Let's begin with the question of whether one must always follow rituals. A passage in the *Mengzi* speaks directly to this topic:

Chunyu Kun asked, "Does ritual require that men and women do not touch when handing something to one another?"

Mengzi replied, "That is the ritual."

Chunyu Kun then asked, "If your sister-in-law were drowning, would you pull her out with your hand?"

Mengzi said, "Only a beast would not pull out his sister-in-law if she were drowning. It is the ritual that men and women should not touch when handing something to one another, but if your sister-in-law is drowning, to pull her out with your hand is a matter of discretion."[4]

The question, then, is how exactly do ritual and "discretion" relate to one another. Who decides when discretion is called for, and does it mean that the ritual is completely overridden? If we update Mengzi's example, answers to these questions will be evident. Instead of a drowning sister-in-law, imagine that you are a college professor and a student in your class needs CPR.[5] The rituals governing professor–student touching are quite clear: no putting your lips against a student's, no putting your hands on his or her chest.[6] In an emergency, though, we would all agree that the right action is to give CPR. Notice, though, that discretion in this case does not give one free rein to ignore the ritual entirely. Touching is okay, but only in the specific ways required for CPR, and only as long as the student requires it. Discretion is thus an ability to balance potentially competing values: how much adherence to the ritual and how much violation of the ritual (out of compassion for the person in jeopardy)? The core meaning of the word I'm translating as "discretion" in fact is "weighing," and we always may be called upon to weigh different concerns and figure out how to balance them. A central message of this chapter is that rituals matter a lot, more than most of us realize today; but my present point is that there still are situations in which rituals can be temporarily, partly outweighed.

Can rituals be changed altogether? We will shortly see why the answer is "yes," but it is worth dwelling for a moment on why it makes sense for rituals to resist changing too easily. Even though the details of specific rituals are sometimes written down—as in a book designed to teach people etiquette—rituals exist not in the pages of any text but in the lived social practices of real communities. Unlike laws, which are created, changed, or eliminated according to explicit procedures, there are no similar processes for rituals. Much like traditions, rituals are handed down from generation to generation; they derive their authority in large part from the authority of a community's elders. They resist change, then, because part of their point is to do things as our ancestors have done them. Nonetheless, rituals can and do change. Sometimes this is a matter of gradual evolution; sometimes it is more intentional. In all cases, Confucians stand ready to assess these changes— endorsing some, rejecting others—based on their understanding of the deeper significance of rituals. As we have seen, rituals are not simply the repetition of earlier patterns. Rituals discipline and ultimately transform us so that we can grow as moral beings and our communities can flourish.

There is plenty of historical evidence that Confucians indeed viewed rituals in this way. Within the *Analects* itself, Kongzi is generally quite conservative regarding ritual change, but both recognizes that rituals differed from one early dynasty to the next, and also explicitly endorses one modification (because, it seems, the change doesn't affect the underlying point of that particular ritual).[7] Subsequent Confucians who live in societies dramatically different from that of Kongzi naturally face questions about change. Zhu Xi, for example, explains that he compiles ancient ritual texts simply in order to facilitate his contemporaries' deciding which of the rituals can be employed in his day, not in order to advocate a return to ancient ways; and he explicitly invokes the classical text "Evolution of Rituals" and its idea that it is fine to invent new rituals so long as they "spring from righteousness."[8] Throughout its long history, the Confucian tradition has certainly known some strongly conservative voices who view ritual less flexibly than does Zhu Xi, but the logic of Zhu's position is compelling and I join with other contemporary Confucians who emphasize the need for critical reflection on our rituals.[9]

Two potential problems remain. On the one hand, we might agree that rituals *can* change, but not be satisfied with the ways in which they *have* changed. For example, although Zhu Xi argued for flexibility and innovation, in some ways the rituals that he endorsed made things worse for women. Answers to this type of challenge must be made in a case-by-case way; we'll look at the reasons modern Confucianism should embrace gender equality in Chapter 18. On the other hand, even if rituals are sufficiently flexible, one might still worry that *any* ritual is likely to be problematic because of the ways that rituals are inherently bound together with class, gender, and other hierarchies that many today find objectionable. As Olberding puts it, we might think that from the perspective of today, rituals are "little more than artifacts of bygone eras, reminders of a time when conventions regarding respect for others were too tightly fused with symbolic markers of social class."[10] More broadly, she remarks that "what societies have historically counted 'dirty,' 'unseemly,' or 'disgusting' has often been turned against their populations' less powerful members," much as hand holding or a goodbye kiss may still evoke disgust in some places if the lovers share the same gender or are of different races.[11] Are rituals inevitably compromised by their entanglement with power and hierarchy?

Imagine that you have just opened a door and begun proceeding, when you notice someone coming up behind you, apparently intent on entering through the same doorway. What do you do? At the time and place that I grew up, boys and men were expected to hold doors open for girls and women, including hurrying ahead to open the door for a female in front of you. Officially, this was meant to express "respect," but one doesn't have to think very hard about this ritual to see that certain kinds of male superiority seem to be implicit in the practice. Once such assumptions have been laid bare, though, what does one do? The options seem to be three: carry on as before (perhaps insisting to anyone who asks that one means nothing derogatory by it), stop holding doors open for anyone, or hold doors open for everyone (while abandoning the practice of hurrying ahead to anticipate the needs of women in front of one). Historically, Confucians were quite tone-deaf to issues of gender oppression; as such, a premodern Confucian would probably advocate the first option. After all, the ritual involves paying attention to the presence of others and helps to strengthen human relationships by expressing a modest kind of deference to others' needs. A modern Confucian, though, would have recognized that once one removes the blinders imposed by ubiquitous patriarchy, Confucians have powerful means to see and critique gender-based oppression. The best answer is therefore the third—egalitarian door-holding—which both preserves the values of the ritual while removing the patriarchal stigma.[12]

To sum up, I have said there are three dimensions to how we should think about ritual: what one does, how one does it, and the effects it has. The "what" is the rules or scripts of socially taught and enforced ritual. The "how" will sometimes come naturally and sometimes require effort; the more obvious the effort, the less "propriety" one is expressing and the more one may be undermining the point of the ritual. Thus, one "effect" that we can hope for is to become more fluid at rituals over time: that is, developing the virtue of propriety. No doubt, we all must force ourselves to follow rituals at least some of the time, but rituals still help to make more constructive interactions possible. One of the most basic things that we can each do to live a more Confucian life is to follow rituals.

5 | CULTIVATE YOUR SPROUTS

Stories about psychopaths are fascinating even as they terrify. Countless movies and novels portray their evils, but part of what captivates us about a character like Dr. Hannibal Lecter of *Silence of the Lambs* is how alien he seems. He is brilliant but so cold—apparently lacking any empathy or emotional connection to other people. How can human communities thrive or even survive with members like Dr. Lecter?

In some ways the opposite question arises when thinking about the lives of non-human animals. The gifted primatologist Frans de Waal has spent his career showing us that animals can have rich emotional and cognitive lives; he titles a recent book *Mama's Last Hug* in honor of a dying chimpanzee matriarch's farewell to her longtime caretaker.[1] Hollywood, at least, is convinced: the many *Planet of the Apes* movies depend on the plausibility of apes sharing emotional ties with one another that mirror those found among humans.

Keep these psychopathic humans and empathic apes in mind as you read the following passage from *Mengzi*:

Suppose someone suddenly saw a child about to fall into a well. Anyone in such a situation would have a feeling of alarm and commiseration—not because they sought to get in good with the child's parents, not because they wanted a good reputation among their neighbors and friends, and not because they would dislike the sounds of the child's cries. From this we can see that if one is without the feeling of alarm and commiseration, one is not human. If one is without the feeling of disdain, one is not human. If one is without the feeling of deference, one is not human. If one is without the feeling of approval and disapproval, one is not human. The feeling of alarm and commiseration is the sprout of humaneness. The feeling of disdain is the sprout of righteousness. The feeling of deference is the sprout of propriety. The feeling of approval and disapproval is the sprout of wisdom. A person having these four sprouts is like their having four limbs.[2]

We don't often encounter uncovered wells today, but just imagine seeing a child chase a ball into a street with an on-coming car: wouldn't you feel "alarm and commiseration"? Mengzi claims that this automatic response, which he also calls the "sprout of humaneness," helps to define who is human.

One set of questions you might have about this passage concerns the other three "sprouts," but let's put those off for the time being. Instead, consider how a psychopath like Dr. Lecter would respond to seeing a baby about to fall into a well. Presumably his very first, spontaneous reaction would be: nothing. We might also imagine that his blazing intellect would rapidly step in for his frozen-solid emotions, and he might soon react with (feigned) alarm or even reach out to save the child. But these actions would precisely be caused by some calculation such as "wanting a good reputation." Mengzi would thus conclude that Dr. Lecter "is not human"—and I think that most of us would agree. The question is not biological ("Is he a *homo sapiens*?") but rather has to do with identity and ethics: "Is he one of us?" The alienness of a true psychopath threatens the most basic foundations for our shared lives, which is the reason it is natural to call someone like Dr. Lecter a "monster."

What about the chimpanzee matriarch Mama? Supposing, as seems very plausible, that she responded with alarm and commiseration upon seeing a baby chimp in danger, does that make her a "human" (or perhaps we should say "person")? Not necessarily. After all, Mengzi has said that those without the sprout are *not* human, but not that those with the sprout *are* human. (Philosophers would say that the sprout is a "necessary" but not "sufficient" condition for being a human.) This matters because the sprout is, well, just a sprout. Like the plants on which the metaphor is based, it needs to be cultivated and so grow into a specific kind of maturity. Without such cultivation, we humans would remain morally immature; human society under such an assumption might resemble chimpanzee society. Confucians like Mengzi aspire to much more.

* * *

Later in the chapter I will return to the question of cultivation, but for now let's focus on the idea of sprouts and more generally on the topic of human nature. We immediately run into a difficulty, because Confucians famously disagreed with one another on the topic of our nature. Mengzi held that nature was "good"; Xunzi argued that it was "bad"; and Neo-Confucians like Zhu Xi and Wang Yangming had their own distinctive and complex views. The job of historians of philosophy is to carefully analyze these differences. My task here is different, because from the standpoint of a contemporary thinker and practitioner, there is tremendous value in being able to draw on insights from across the tradition. And on balance, the tradition has embraced the idea that we have a deep, positive orientation. It needs to be cultivated but we do have a starting point. Xunzi is right to be worried about what results from leaving things to develop on their own, but our starting point is not as bare and directionless as he thinks. Furthermore, modern science concurs.

Confucians throughout the tradition agree that at any given stage of life, we respond to stimuli with a range of different kinds of affective (that is, related to feeling) reactions. They also agree that in principle, any of these reactions can be appropriate and good. Responding to hunger by desiring to eat can be apt or it can go awry; responding to a provocation with anger can be apt or it can go awry; and so on. Just to be clear: even sages can and should be angry or sad or pleased; it just has to be to the right degree and under the right circumstances. What about sprouts like "alarm and commiseration": Can they go awry? Here Confucians did not always agree, but it seems like the answer might be "yes." Cringing when your child faces even the most minor challenge or suffers even the tiniest harm might be bad for you, be bad for the child, and send the wrong signals to others as well.[3]

Another point of consensus within the tradition is that we begin life with a set of emotional dispositions (that is, patterns of affective response) that will lead us into trouble if we do nothing to shape how they change over time. Xunzi is the most explicit about this, writing:

> People's nature is such that they are born with a fondness for profit in them. If they follow along with this, then struggle and contention will arise, and yielding and deference will perish therein. They are born with feelings of hate and dislike in them. If they follow along with these, then cruelty and villainy will arise, and loyalty and trustworthiness will perish therein. They are born with desires of the eyes and ears, a fondness for beautiful sights and sounds. If they follow along with these, then lasciviousness and chaos will arise, and ritual and righteousness, proper form and order, will perish therein.[4]

Note that Xunzi does not say that fondness for profit and so on are bad in themselves; if we "follow along" with them, though, the consequences are dire. Mengzi also understands that our untutored emotions can be problematic. The moral "sprouts" are initially weak and—at least until they have grown to robust maturity—are vulnerable to being worn down by social pressures.[5] At the same time, our more neutral, physical desires (like "fondness for beautiful sights and sounds") can easily draw us into trouble if they are left on their own. As Mengzi says, "The senses of hearing and seeing do not reflect and are obscured by external things."[6] "Reflection," we shall see later, is part of how we put our physical desires into a broader context and steer ourselves on a moral course.

For their part, the later Neo-Confucians understand our complex psycho-physical reactions through the category of "vital stuff." "Vital stuff" is a fascinating, inclusive category that makes up all the things in the cosmos and refers both to their material states and their tendencies. Is someone tall? That is explained by her vital stuff. Growing is a matter of vital stuff changing. Does he tend to feel awkward in social situations? Or perhaps she is irascible, feeling angry at the slightest provocation? All these are results of the particular configurations of vital stuff. We nowadays understand things like temperament and health to be complicated interactions between our material and psychological selves, to say nothing of what physicists tell us about the relation between matter and energy. So, it may not seem like too much of a stretch to use an all-encompassing category like "vital stuff." At any rate, Neo-Confucians explain all our tendencies to desire too much, care too little, or otherwise respond poorly to the world's stimuli by saying that one's vital stuff is impure or imbalanced; it is the job of education and cultivation to purify or balance out one's vital stuff.[7]

So, all Confucians agree that any given person has tendencies of emotional responsiveness, that these tendencies are often quite flawed, and that the tendencies can be improved. One important corollary of these beliefs is that badness comes from a lack of sufficient goodness, or an imbalance among tendencies that are on their own neutral (or even good), rather than from a source that is itself inherently bad. Badness, even evil, can result from overflowing desires that are not limited, cultivated, or re-directed; but there is nothing like an innate, sadist sprout. Even Hannibal Lecter is not intrinsically evil: he lacks positive moral emotions and has allowed his desires to develop unchecked. Not only is badness not inherent in us, but most Confucians explicitly add that there is an orientation toward goodness built into our tendencies (at least those who are "human"). For Mengzi, these are the sprouts, about which we will discuss more in a moment. For Neo-Confucians, goodness is rooted in their conception of our "nature" in a different sense. They hold that the natures of humans and indeed of all things have implicit structures: deep-seated orientations toward balanced interdependence and never-ending embrace of life.

Let me pause here to reflect on what we modern humans with our understanding of evolutionary science should make of this Neo-Confucian notion of "nature." Perhaps we might agree that science confirms the idea of interdependence. From microscale (like the bacteria that must flourish in our guts for us to be healthy) to macro-scale (like climate change), we see evidence everywhere that health, flourishing, even life itself depends on countless connections to other entities. And the idea that continued life and reproduction are deep, driving factors is of course also easy for us to accept today. It is the further claim that our natures orient us toward "balanced" or "harmonious" interdependence that modern science might challenge. What about the survival of the fittest, "nature red in tooth and claw"?

A modern-day inheritor of Neo-Confucian ideas has three ways of responding to this challenge. First, developments in evolutionary theory have shown that the Darwinian picture of competition for survival is mistaken in many ways; cooperation can often be found in nature. Still, we cannot conclude that modern evolutionary science has completely replaced "competition" with "harmony." Second, the idea of vital stuff can readily account for selfish or egoistic drives to pursue one's own life at the expense of others. Third, and most important, we can come to see that selfish drives toward "success" are partial, short-term, and therefore un-reliable. In fact, our concern with life is not just a drive toward re-production (no matter what role that plays in the development of our biology), but a caring for life; and this care—or love—is what grounds the claim that our natures orient us toward harmonious interdependence. The Neo-Confucian idea that we are implicitly oriented toward the caring embrace of life is powerful and yet con-troversial, even among Confucians today. I will draw on it more than once later in the book and ask readers to keep an open mind for now.

For now, let us return to Mengzi's idea of sprouts. Is it possible that Mengzi was correct when he observed more than two thou-sand years ago that we have distinct, nascent moral feelings that can be grown into full-fledged virtues? The best answer to this ques-tion comes from the contemporary philosopher Owen Flanagan. Flanagan has spent his career seeking to bridge two chasms: that between philosophy and psychology, and that between Western philosophy and Eastern philosophical traditions like Buddhism and Confucianism. In his book *The Geography of Morals*, Flanagan demonstrates that Mengzi's "sprout theory" resembles many modern theories about the "modularity" of human pre-moral "first nature": that is, both Mengzi and modern scholars think that we begin with certain proto-moral dispositions, which are both relevant to but different from a fully developed, moral "second nature."[8] For Mengzi, the sprouts are alarm and commiseration, deference, disdain, and approval and disapproval; for a modern scholar like Jonathan Haidt, they are care, reciprocity, loyalty, respect, and sanctity.[9] Flanagan explores the differences between these models and argues that the general idea is very plausible, even if our sprouts are almost certainly incomplete, changing, and interpenetrating as we grow in ways that Mengzi never made explicit.[10]

Summing up where things stand, there is a range of things that talk of "sprouts" or "nature" mean for Confucians, and there are certainly questions about how these various ideas interface with modern evolutionary and psychological theories. One of the things that living as a Confucian today might mean—for some but not all—is to more deeply investigate these matters, in conversation with scholars like Flanagan. No matter where these scholarly investigations lead, the practical implications of most Confucian views are very similar. We need to do sustained work on ourselves in order most fully to realize the moral potential that is hinted at by our sprouts. This is the project of cultivation.

* * *

According to Mengzi, if one works at cultivation, one's sprouts can grow into full-fledged virtues. In fact, Mengzi concludes the sprout passage by saying:

> Having these four sprouts within oneself, if one knows to fill them all out, it will be like a fire starting up or a spring breaking through! If one can merely fill them all out, they will be sufficient to care for all within the Four Seas. If one merely

fails to fill them out, they will be insufficient to serve one's parents.[11]

Cultivation is work, but once the sprouts grow into full-fledged virtues (that is, once you "fill them out"), the resulting capabilities are powerful and automatic. This is why Confucians describe the virtuous reactions of a sage as spontaneous. We'll soon be exploring specific kinds of Confucian cultivation: listening, reading, reflecting, attending, and engaging. To set the stage, let's begin with a more general question about the relation between our sprouts and their cultivation, namely, Why should we bother? Is there something about our nature that requires it?

Earlier we saw that Confucian teachings aim to build on, shape, and cultivate what we already are. In the passage we have just seen from Mengzi, he points out that if one does not fill out one's sprouts, those sprouts "will be insufficient to serve one's parents." After all, genuinely and effectively caring for one's parents requires more than feeling badly if they are about to fall into a well; as we saw in Chapter 3, it even requires more than providing them with food and shelter. Among other things, it means being perceptive about and responsive to their needs, and to do so in a way that respects their experience and authority. Mengzi's key insight is that as a matter of fact, there are vital concerns that we have for one another and only with work can we become people who reliably answer to these concerns. To refuse to cultivate oneself is to deny oneself.

The motivation to cultivate, then, can be seen to come from twin aspects of the way we experience the world. On the one hand, it does not take much attention to one's world to experience unease at the disharmony all around one—starting with challenges one's parents are facing, perhaps, and then extending out from there. On the other hand, Confucians point to experiences that show us the nascent possibility of unobstructed harmony: of everything fitting together, everything making sense. Mengzi tends to concentrate on the former, negative sort of motivation, as when he writes that King Wu took it as a personal affront if there was a single bully in the empire.[12] Neo-Confucians have more to say about the latter, for example, by emphasizing moments of clarity when everything seems right with the world. Taken together, these experiences can both push us to change ourselves and our world and pull us toward better versions of each.

Admittedly, we usually experience these pushes and pulls as rather weak, compared to the powerful attraction of selfish consumerism, for example, and so it is important that there are two other types of motivation for cultivation. First, some types of cultivation are largely outside of one's control. Children have little choice but to engage in the rituals that their elders demand of them, and social norms keep the pressure on adults as well. So insofar as rituals go beyond simply disciplining our behavior to transforming our dispositions (or our vital stuff, as the Neo-Confucians would say), this can work without a conscious motivation. Second, cultivation is rarely a solo endeavor. From families to friendships to schools to workplaces, there are many contexts in which people can encourage one another to try harder and help each other when they are struggling; this fact leads one contemporary Confucian philosopher to characterize society as "a community of learners."[13] In a wonderful autobiography, a 15th-century Neo-Confucian clearly experiences both pushes and pulls: he writes of anxiety and shame, but also regularly makes remarks like, "How lovely it is today to behold the vital impulse of all the various plants!" Furthermore, he recognizes the benefits of having what we might call a training partner: after ten days in which he felt his efforts flagging, he writes, "Now where can I find a good friend to help me realize this ambition of mine to reach sagehood?"[14]

This discussion of human nature has contained some of the densest discussion of the whole book, but let's not lose sight of the core idea. We humans have a rich and flexible "nature" that includes key "sprouts" that can be cultivated into full-fledged, powerful moral tendencies. Mama the chimpanzee has some but not all of the potential that we humans have, which is why Confucians—some of whom were very observant about other animals' social tendencies—think that only humans can actually become sages. A psychopath like Dr. Lecter lacks the sprouts entirely, but thankfully the vast majority of us are not Hannibal Lecter. In fact, we're generally somewhere along the path of nurturing our sprouts; the more we can cultivate them, the closer we get to a fully virtuous life.

Some of the Confucians' deepest insights have to do with how to do this: how we can grow more moral. Many aspects of our education and everyday lives can contribute, from reading to music to reflection to political engagement. Yes, even listening to music can help to make you a better person!

6 | READ IN THE RIGHT WAY

Good teachers, frustrated by societies that are obsessed with shallow ideas of success, can be counted on to resist "teaching to the test" and instead to try and guide their students toward more meaningful learning. Consider the words of one such teacher:

> The books you read should be embodied in your person. I don't know whether what you routinely study is on your mind at all times or not. But if it isn't, you're just hurrying through the texts, reading for their literal meaning and taking little pleasure in them. This, I fear, will be of no benefit to you in the end.

These words could easily have been directed at students almost anywhere in the world today who are preparing for a college entrance exam. In fact, they were said by Zhu Xi in the 12th century.[1] Many of his students were as test-obsessed as their modern counterparts. They sought to do well on the Civil Service Exams which were the keys to entering the vaunted imperial bureaucracy, but Zhu warned them that how and what you study has significance far beyond the score you get on the test. Building on the ideas of his Confucian forebears, Zhu had fascinating ideas about why reading is important and how to do it well.

* * *

Kongzi loved the *Odes*. A collection of ancient poems and song lyrics, the *Odes* comes up repeatedly in the *Analects*. Kongzi doesn't simply read it for pleasure, though; he finds that it leads him to deeper insights, which in turn inspires growth. Consider this exchange with his student Zixia about one such poem:

ZIXIA ASKED: "Oh, her artful smile is dimpled. / Oh, her beautiful eye is black and white. / Oh, a plain background on which to apply the highlights." What does this refer to?

THE MASTER SAID: In painting, everything follows the plain background.

ZIXIA SAID: Does ritual follow similarly?

THE MASTER SAID: Zixia, you have inspired me! Finally I have someone with whom to discuss the *Odes*.[2]

There are at least a couple things we can take away from this curious conversation. First, Kongzi's focus is not on the beauty of the language or images, but on the meaning, relevance, and effects of the poem. Second, by approaching the *Odes* in the right way, one can learn things and be inspired.

To read in the right way, it is not enough just to be on the lookout for deep meanings. I am reminded of myself as a freshman in college. I am afraid I was a frustrating student for my literature professors, as I was always impatient to get to the meaning, the point, the philosophical issue that I wanted to discuss. On at least one occasion, I am embarrassed to say, I enthusiastically debated the meaning of *Emma* without having read even a word of it. (In my partial defense, I had a *lot* of reading that semester and it was very hard to keep up!) Several Confucians talk about the necessity of deep and repeated reading, rather than superficial acquaintance; perhaps Zhu Xi is most explicit, as we see in this passage:

> In reading, students should keep to these three rules: (1) read little but become intimately familiar with what you read; (2) don't scrutinize the text, developing your own far-fetched views of it, but rather personally experience it over and over again; (3) concentrate fully, without thought of gain.[3]

For an example of whom Zhu Xi would no doubt approve, instead of my freshman self we should look to the 15th-century Confucian Wu Yubi, who recorded his struggles—and successes—with Confucian learning in a marvelous, life-long journal. At one point he writes:

> This evening, slowly walking through the fields, I was silently chanting passages from *Doctrine of the Mean*. I took my time, going over each word and phrase, chanting them with great feeling. Realized in my heartmind, verified by my experience, this book has given me a great deal of insight.[4]

Wu is not just finding whatever he wants in the text of *Doctrine of the Mean*: the words of the text have real authority. As he puts it elsewhere, "Only by constantly settling the heartmind down by reading books will it not be overwhelmed by external things."[5]

Let's pause briefly to think about the word *xin*, which I am translating as "heartmind." Western traditions have long emphasized the distinction between reason, associated with mind or soul, and feelings, associated with the heart or body. Plato goes so far as to argue that pure reasoning is impossible as long as one's soul is connected to a body, so philosophers should be prepared to die (which sets their immortal souls free). Chinese traditions take another approach. Thinking and feelings are understood to be interrelated, both housed in the same "place," the *xin*. Physically, this is the organ that we label the "heart," and so *xin* is often translated as heart. But because the *xin* is also the seat of thought and reflection, it's better to emphasize the connections between thinking and feeling by rendering it "heartmind."

Now return to Wu Yubi's chanting words "with great feeling." Lest you think that the Confucians are calling on us to have a weirdly worshipful attitude toward the printed word, let's look at a few qualifications. Mengzi says:

> . . . in explaining an ode, one should not allow the words to obscure the sentence, nor the sentence to obscure the author's commitment. The right way to get it is to use one's righteousness to meet the author's commitment.[6]

This is a fascinating and rich passage that commentators have not always understood, sometimes focusing too narrowly on what they see as the "meaning" that an author wants to convey. But Mengzi's point is not about meanings and how to interpret texts: it is about how to learn from texts in a deeper sense. Success comes to the extent that one is able to grasp and internalize the moral "commitment" that an author is expressing through the words on the page.[7] This is why meeting the author's commitment with one's own—that is, with one's sense of "righteousness," in Mengzi's terms—is the right way to experience the text. This is presumably why Kongzi says that one should "find inspiration in the *Odes*."[8] Don't just learn about good ideas: be inspired! Inspiration isn't a matter of knowledge, but of changed attitude.

Let's now pause to think about why books by or about exemplars are able to inspire us. Confucians believe it is because reading can call our attention to things already inside us. Neo-Confucians, as we saw in Chapter 5, hold that our natures have deep-seated orientations toward balanced interdependence and never-ending embrace of life. Thus, Zhu Xi can write:

> Book learning is of secondary importance. It would seem that Pattern is originally complete in people; the reason we must engage in book learning is that we have not experienced much. The sages experienced a great deal and wrote it down for others to read. Now in book learning we must simply apprehend the many manifestations of Pattern.[9]

Other Confucians before and since Zhu Xi may debate about the idea that there is "Pattern . . . originally complete" in us, but most will agree that books can help us to notice our own potential and see how to extend it in the proper ways (as this book and others in the same series try to do!). Whether or not they accept the Neo-Confucian idea of "Pattern," that is, Confucians hold that much about the most fitting ways to live together is objectively discoverable, that insightful authors have been able to capture this in their writings, and therefore that we today can learn from and be motivated by their writings—finding them to resonate with our own "sprouts" of goodness. Zhu Xi's own emphasis tends to be on didactic writings and on poetry, but modern theorists like Martha Nussbaum have helped us to see that novels and shorter fiction can also play similar roles.[10] Still, because the ultimate goal is personal and societal moral growth, book learning itself is of secondary importance, as Zhu Xi says.

A final feature of the Confucian way to read meshes well with the idea that the books themselves are secondary: namely, the open-minded and questioning attitude with which one should read. Speaking of the *Documents* classic, Mengzi says, "It would be better not to have the *Documents* than to believe everything in it."[11] Xunzi notes that because we have "no examples of the Classics' present application," without a teacher to guide one's reading, one "will simply be learning haphazard knowledge and focusing one's intention on blindly following the *Odes* and the *Documents*."[12] But this does not mean that we must simply blindly follow our teachers; as a contemporary scholar says about Xunzian education: "The training aims at producing capable, refined, sensitive judgment and understanding as the backbone of expert practical ability in ritual and other Confucian arts. Questioning and even challenging one's teacher appears to be a perfectly acceptable way to seek greater understanding."[13]

For his part, Zhu Xi stresses the importance of questioning and doubt over and over. In fact, in one passage we can see that he kept an open mind about the best way to "doubt" and eventually revised his views, preferring an "open mind" to forced doubting:

> In the past, I taught my friends to seek points of doubt when reading books. Recently, I have seen that it is better to study with an open mind. After lengthy, careful reading, we will naturally get some of the material, and have doubts about some. Upon a close reading, we will encounter things that block our path and cause us to be perplexed. Thus doubts will naturally arise, prompting us to compare, weigh, and reflect on those matters.[14]

Importantly, Zhu says that an open mind involves questioning our own understandings as much as those of others:

> One weakness among people is that they only know how to doubt the explanations of others, but do not know how to question their own explanations. If people would try to critique themselves as they criticize others, then they will come close to realizing their own successes and failures.[15]

Reading in the right way will lead us to grow as moral beings, inspired to be closer to the sages, in part because of seeing the deep similarities between the sages and ourselves.

* * *

Or so the Confucians say. Nonetheless, you may be wondering: How can such an approach to reading avoid falling into either rigid scholasticism or anything-goes subjectivism? And what relevance does this have in the present day?

Scholasticism is a narrow focus on the texts of a specific canon; scholastics devote themselves with ever-increasing levels of technical sophistication to interpreting details of the texts. Subjectivism tells us to embrace whatever an individual finds in a text: it is up to each person's "subjectivity" to articulate what is of value to that person. In contemporary academic parlance, any "reading" of a text is valid. No one could read Zhu Xi's extended teachings about reading—nor indeed, the thoughts on reading of pretty much any Confucian—and come away thinking that they embrace scholasticism or subjectivism. Yet as a matter of historical fact, China saw quite a lot of each. Some scholars even went beyond scholasticism and called for the active suppression of alternative sets of texts.[16] How do we make sense of this?

It is always a challenge to institutionalize an approach to education that relies at its core on balance and judgment. There is no single or obvious criterion of genuine success for Confucian reading because moral growth is hard to measure. Psychologists are actively studying how to assess moral development, but this is a very contested area of research. More generally, it is difficult not to sympathize with Zhu Xi's frustration over the ways in which education in the Classics in his day was so often just a matter of memorization and regurgitation, and what passed for scholarship on the Classics was unthinking scholasticism. Zhu himself wrote commentaries and advocated a particular curriculum, but he explained that this was to make it easier for teachers and students to approach education in the right way, by beginning with texts that lent themselves to inspirational and accessible moral learning before moving on to others. He explicitly says that it is fine to read anything ("There are no books that shouldn't be read"[17]), though more "superficial" texts do not need to be read in the intensive way that I have been discussing in this chapter.[18]

As for subjectivism, we can sharpen the question by asking whether we are confident that Kongzi and Zixia were right about the meaning of the ode I quoted toward the beginning of this chapter. Is the "commitment" of the poet truly revealed when Zixia makes a connection between the application of cosmetics and the basis of ritual? To answer this question, we must be cautious about *to whom* something is being revealed. When you or I read the passage, it may leave us cold, mystified, or even bemused. Some critics have charged that there is no such meaning to be found in the poem, while another suggests that this is simply the application of the "liberal hermeneutic that was standard" at the time: a good reading of an ode is one that is "both instructive and unapparent."[19] This is certainly not what the passage itself is telling us, though. Rather, reflection on this ode together with Kongzi's comment sparked in Zixia a resonance, a recognition of how ritual practices relate to his own psychology; and his wise teacher is able to see that this recognition is genuine (in part because of the way it matches up with Kongzi's own, cultivated sense of the world). Had Zixia said, "I see!—our natures are blank like a plain canvas," Kongzi would likely have frowned and turned away. A reading is successful when one is "inspired," which is of course subjective in one sense: one has to get it oneself. But this is very different from saying that anything goes.

Given the challenges the Confucians faced historically at implementing this kind of reading in educational institutions—remember Zhu Xi's laments about "teaching to the test" in his day—it is natural to wonder about its significance today. One data point comes from a student in the very first class I taught on Neo-Confucianism. Part-way through the semester, she approached me after a class on some of Zhu Xi's ideas. "I really enjoyed today's discussion," she said. "I feel that this is the most relevant course that I have taken in college." My first reaction was shock and a little dismay; medieval Neo-Confucianism is the most relevant class she has taken?! What does this say about the role of liberal education in our society? But as we chatted, I came to see that what she meant was that reading Zhu and probing what he meant was speaking to her in a deep way. In class that day I had asked the students to think of some conflict, large or small, that had occurred with their roommates, and then to talk about how they might understand it differently, or react differently, if we were to take an idea like "Pattern" seriously. As far as I could tell, this was the first time in her life that she had ever done something like this in a structured way. While I wouldn't go so far as to say she was becoming Confucian, she was definitely thinking about what "learning" meant in a new way.

Asking students to take the texts they read seriously and even to undertake "experiments in living" (the final project in some of my classes involves choosing a text from the semester and seeking to live in accord with it for five days) fits well with the need that

Michael Roth has identified for liberal education to be more than "critical thinking" and for our students to be more than "self-satisfied debunkers." He writes:

> In campus cultures where being smart means being a critical unmasker, students may become too good at showing how things can't possibly make sense. They may close themselves off from their potential to find or create meaning and direction from the books, music and experiments they encounter in the classroom.[20]

Roth does not want to dispense with criticism—and neither, we should remember, do Zhu Xi and his fellow Confucians—but he worries that over the last half century, the student's role as inquirer "has taken the guise of the sophisticated (often ironic) spectator, rather than the messy participant in continuing experiments or even the reverent beholder of great cultural achievements."

Roth's invocation of "great cultural achievements" brings me to my final question. Roth and Zhu Xi find common cause in endorsing what we today call the "humanities." Science, technology, and materialistic progress have their place, but so do the humanities if we are to value living not merely well-off but actually good lives. As we have just seen, Roth and Zhu Xi would also concur that the goal of reading cannot simply be debunking. But when we speak of "great cultural achievements" is there a risk of fetishizing the past—a past, furthermore, that was characterized by sexism, racism, and many other exclusions? Kongzi famously said that he "transmits rather than invents"; is it any wonder that defenders of "the Western tradition" in the United States today tend to be conservative, male, and white?

My response is that the Confucianism recommended in this book is a progressive Confucianism—a Confucianism that, in its efforts to help us and our societies get better, self-critically recognizes that it, too, must respond to changing circumstances. In a similar vein, philosopher Martha Nussbaum argues that any effort to find value in the ancients must also pay attention to the importance of history. She writes that "we cannot see how to bring timeless standards of goodness to our own society unless we have understood what possibilities historical change have made available to human beings at different times and in different places."[21] Such a historical consciousness enables us to see the importance of not only the similarities but also the differences between Zhu Xi's society and our own. Zhu criticized teaching to the test, but his students were all men, mostly from elite families. Confucians today must therefore be open-minded and inclusive as we develop our curricula, reading insights from many sources and stories about a diverse range of exemplars. After all, it is only such a process of broadening that has led to Zhu Xi's own recent entrance into the American philosophical curriculum!

7 | LISTEN TO THE RIGHT MUSIC

On August 18, 1969, rock guitarist Jimi Hendrix brought his set—and the entire Woodstock music festival—to a close by playing the US national anthem, "The Star-Spangled Banner." This extraordinary performance has since been described by music critic Charles Shaar Murray as "probably the most complex and powerful work of American art to deal with the Vietnam War"[1]; if you have access to the Internet right now, I recommend heading straight to YouTube and watching the video before reading any further. Murray paints this picture of the song:

> That clear, pure tone—somewhere between a trumpet and a high, pealing bell—is continually invaded by ghostly rogue overtones; the stately unreeling of the melody derailed by the sounds of riot and war, sirens and screams, riots and alarms; Hendrix presented a compelling musical allegory of a nation bloodily tearing itself apart, in its own ghettos and campuses, and in a foreign land which had never done anything to harm its tormentors.[2]

Hendrix also weaves in a few bars of "Taps," the tune traditionally played on a bugle at US military funerals, in a mark of respect and a nod to his own time as a member of the 101st Airborne Division (though he was never in Vietnam).

Predictably, not everyone was thrilled with Hendrix's rendition of the national anthem. Writing about a slightly later performance, an *L.A. Times* critic said that it was "meaningless and constitutes the cheapest kind of sensationalism."[3] Hendrix was even threatened with physical harm if he dared to play it at a concert in Dallas.[4] Such threats attest to the power of the music, suggesting that the *L.A. Times* critic was obviously wrong in ascribing no meaning to Hendrix's playing. Indeed, in an interview Hendrix himself responds to the question of whether music has meaning by saying:

> Oh, yeah, definitely. It's getting to be more spiritual than anything now. Pretty soon I believe that they're going to have to rely on music to get some kind of peace of mind or satisfaction—direction actually—more so than politics, because politics is really on an ego scene.[5]

Politics, Hendrix worries, has lost the ability to guide people because it no longer has a moral core: it is just about individuals seeking their own selfish interests.

Kongzi, too, thought that music was meaningful and powerful, especially in its ability to unite and sustain community—so much so that he advocated banning certain kinds of music which he felt were having bad effects on his society. What, then, should

Confucians today make of Jimi Hendrix's "The Star-Spangled Banner"? More generally, must Confucians join with the cultural conservatives who criticize rock and other popular music as corrupting the young? To the contrary: for music to unite and shape us in healthy ways, it must draw upon the cultures of the diverse members of contemporary communities, while at the same time expressing values at the heart of Confucianism. For a modern American, this means that Jimi Hendrix's rendition of the national anthem is exemplary Confucian music-making.

* * *

Confucians often pair ritual and music. Each is a powerful technology whose prudent use can encourage moral growth and help to shape a harmonious society. Recall that ritual gives us ways to express our feelings through a kind of shorthand, disciplines us by tamping down or channeling our emotions, and contributes to changing our long-term dispositions. Music has functions similar to each of these dimensions of ritual. Singing, playing music, or even just choosing to listen to a certain song can all express our feelings. Attending to the music someone is making can tell us a lot about their state of mind—or even, according to Kongzi, the state of an entire society.[6] The short-term influences music has on us (akin to ritual's "disciplining") are perhaps its most obvious functions. In these days of streaming services, I listen to much of my music via Apple Music, often enough by choosing a "Mood": Do I want "Focus" or "Fitness," "Feel Good" or "Chill," "Blue" or "Romance"? As Xunzi says, "Music enters into people deeply and transforms people quickly": there is little question that the right music can nudge us to feel one way or another, often quite quickly and powerfully.[7]

The idea that music can cultivate us more deeply may be more controversial, but this is its most important power—and the main reason why (as Xunzi says) "the former kings were cautious in creating patterns for it."[8] Another text invokes Kongzi as having said, "For altering mores and changing customs, nothing is better than music."[9] As we assess this claim, it will be important to keep in mind that the "music" (*yue*) about which Kongzi was speaking is not merely organized sound, but consistently refers to a whole package of instrumental music, songs, dance, and other forms of performance.[10] With this in mind, I think we can see two different reasons for following the Confucians here. First, as James Harold points out, there is very good evidence for a related link between repeated exposure to primarily visual, violent media (like movies and video games) and changes in character (specifically, becoming more aggressive).[11] It is plausible that similar effects may come with exposure to various kinds of music—including music videos—although specific research on this question to date is sparse and inconclusive.[12]

Second, early Confucians put particular emphasis on music's ability to "unite," and I think this also ties into its broader power to shape us. One of the most important early Confucian texts about music states that:

> Music serves to unite; ritual serves to differentiate. With uniting there is mutual closeness; with differentiation there is mutual respect. If the deportment of ritual is established, then the noble and the plebeian are separated into classes.

When the patterns of music are uniform, then those in high
position and those in low position get along in harmony."[13]

It is essential to music that different voices or different instruments
harmoniously combine into a whole: they do not compete with
one another for dominance. I played bass for many years in
orchestras and understood that our job was usually not to carry
the melody. This same logic can be extended beyond musicians.
Music unites people when we listen to a performance together and
all the more so when we sing together—for example, singing one's
national anthem at a sporting event. Whereas rituals depend at
least in part in assigning distinct roles (bride, groom, and officiant,
for example), music brings us together.

Music's ability to unite us and sustain community, in turn, gives
it power to shape us. When thinking about how we are "shaped,"
it is easy to imagine that what changes is an entirely internal set
of psychological states, but in fact philosophers and psychologists
today understand that our dispositions come from complex
interactions between individual psychology and social situations.
It is often difficult to draw hard-and-fast distinctions between
inner and outer.[14] Thinking again of the regular, communal
singing of a song like "The Star-Spangled Banner," it seems plausible to expect that the result of participating in such a community
would be to be shaped by it in turn: we become fellow nationals,
patriots even, through such participation. In short, more than just
expressing how we feel or who we are, music actively changes us in
both short-term and long-term ways.

* * *

The core Confucian stance on music can be summed up this way: music is powerful; music is powerful because it affects us in predictable ways, for good or for ill; because it affects us, we should control the music to which we listen. Much of the rest of this chapter will focus on what it can or should mean to "control" music, but first let's think about a possible problem with the argument I just sketched. Perhaps music is really just about form and beauty, not meaning and value. In this case it might affect us in superficial ways but not in ways that connect up with ethics, with virtue, or with social harmony. If so, why should we worry about controlling it?

The question of whether music has ethically relevant meaning is a huge one that cannot be definitively answered here, but we might bear a few things in mind. Remember that "music" does not just mean sounds, but sounds coupled with lyrics, performance, and dance; in a modern context, we can add music videos. So, there are multiple channels along which "music" can carry its meaning. Traditional Confucians also distinguished between the beauty and the morality of music, even if they also felt these dimensions were often related. Kongzi said of Shao music, "It is perfectly beautiful, and also perfectly good," while he said of Wu music, "It is perfectly beautiful, but not perfectly good."[15] In part what Kongzi has in mind is that Shao music (purportedly) comes from the court of Yao, the greatest of sages, while Wu comes from the court of the later and somewhat lesser King Wu; this difference comes out in the messages conveyed by the respective compositions. Significantly, a major difference between Yao and Wu is that only the latter is remembered for engaging in war—albeit, morally justified war aimed at overthrowing a tyrant—and so Wu's music has a martial flair. Finally, remember that no less a musical authority than Jimi Hendrix felt that music was an important source of ethical or political (he actually says "spiritual") meaning.

Let's turn, then, to the question of whether, how much, and how we should try to "control" the music that we and others hear. Kongzi himself was unequivocal: "Abolish the sounds of Zheng, for the sounds of Zheng are lewd,"[16] and "I detest the fact that the sounds of Zheng are corrupting our classical court music."[17] A slightly later Confucian text echoes these same views: "The sounds of Zheng and Wei are the sounds of a chaotic age. It borders on dissoluteness."[18] Notice that these passages do not dignify the music associated with the states of Zheng and Wei with the formal term "music" (*yue*): it is simply "sound."[19] (It is not too hard to imagine a modern parent complaining about the "noise" their children are listening to!)

It is also significant that the texts disparage Zheng music as lewd, corrupting, and dissolute. The criticism is not simply that Zheng music is new, disrupting tradition. Consider the following exchange, which makes clear why Zheng music might be attractive but also problematic:

An official asked the Confucian Zi Xia: "When I put on my official robe and black hat and listen to ancient music (*yue*), I only feel I will keel over from boredom. When I listen to the new music (*yin*) of Zheng and Wei, I do not know what it means to be tired. May I ask, why is ancient music like this and new music like that?"

Zi Xia replied, "With ancient music, the dancers advance and retreat in unison, and the music is made broad with an upright harmony. Instruments of strings, gourds, and reeds are all held together by the rhythm of shakers and drums. The performance begins with the civil (drums) and is again brought to order at the end with the military (bells). At this point, the exemplary person discusses its meaning, and talks about the ancients."

"Now with the new music, the dancers advance and retreat in contracted movements, and the music overflows with lascivious sounds. It entrances the listener and does not cease. It reaches the point of clowns and dwarfs, and boys and girls frolicking together like monkeys, and the distinction between father and son is not known. At the end of the music, no discussion can be done, and the ancients cannot be talked about."[20]

Clearly the problem with Zheng music has to do with the meaning ascribed to its entrancing beats.

Because the concern is about the music's content and not its novelty, then in principle Confucians should be willing to accept changes to music. At least one classical thinker did. Mengzi reassured King Xuan—who was perhaps not the noblest of men but was at least willing to listen to Mengzi and try to improve—that the fact that he was "fond of music" was a sufficient foundation for moral growth, even though the king admitted that he was "unable to enjoy the music of the Former Kings" and only enjoyed "the vulgar music of the present age." Mengzi replies: "If your highness's fondness for music is great, then your state of Qi is almost there! The music of today is like the music of ancient times."[21] He goes on to explain that the key is that all people are able to enjoy music—to satisfy their natural desires for joyous expression and community—and so the king must engage in a "humane politics" that enables the "shared enjoyment" of music. Mengzi later says that "humane sounds" enter people more deeply than "humane words."[22]

Mengzi's flexibility concerning musical novelty is something of an outlier in the Confucian tradition, but this does not mean that his peers would insist on stamping out every trace of popular, possibly "vulgar" music. The contemporary scholar P.J. Ivanhoe suggests that we pay careful attention to the fact that Kongzi was talking about changing the ritualized music in royal courts. He writes: "In our own terms, we might think of someone who would oppose changing the national anthem, or performing a hip-hop version of 'Taps' at the funeral of a fallen soldier."[23] This may be right—and I will return to the national anthem in a moment—but if we take Confucian teachings about music to apply only to extremely formal (akin to a royal court) environments, we may be narrowing things too much. Recalling music's ability to "unite" us despite the different roles assigned to us by rituals, we might also want to consider the main thesis of an article called "Kongzi and Country Music." The author writes that according to Confucians, "the purpose of music is to rejoice in one's social role. Country music constantly exemplifies this function of music."[24] (Consider the refrain of "Domestic Life" by John Conlee: "Living that domestic life / Happy children and a pretty wife / Our Cocker Spaniel's always having puppies / How could anybody be so lucky?") If this is right, though, does that mean that Confucians should criticize changes to the contents of country music, and perhaps also reject any music that does not similarly celebrate traditional social roles?

* * *

Continuity is an important part of how music and rituals function, and well-functioning music and rituals are important parts of Confucian lives. However, music and rituals themselves cannot tell us whether music and rituals should change. Asking whether existing music or rituals need to change is something that one does based on two factors: Does the form of the music or ritual enable it to serve its function, and is the underlying meaning and value still in keeping with the deepest goals of Confucian lives? Although there were some quixotic efforts to reconstruct ancient music during China's subsequent dynasties, many Confucians accepted that the form of music—just like the details of rituals— must change as society, musical technology, and so on change.[25] As we will see, traditional Confucian views of gender are incompatible with the deepest values of Confucianism, and so must be changed; and some other forms of hierarchy are also untenable for modern Confucians. These arguments have consequences for how Confucians today should think about music that, for example, embraces the musical forms of groups that have historically been excluded from mainstream ideas about national or cultural "unity."

The history of performances of "The Star-Spangled Banner" over the last fifty or more years offers a fascinating window on these issues. In 1968, ten months prior to Hendrix's Woodstock performance, the blind, Puerto Rican singer Jose Feliciano gave one of the first non-standard "Banner" performances, before Game 5 of the World Series. His soulful, folk rendition outraged many fans—some of whom booed—even though he later insisted that his goal was to show his appreciation "to America for what they had done for me."[26] By 1983, though, Marvin Gaye sang an R&B rendition of the "Banner" at the NBA Allstar Game that fans applauded and many count among the best performances of the anthem. (Still, the NBA Commissioner at the time was apparently not pleased.[27]) Rap versions of the "Banner" have not gained mainstream acceptance, and at least some of the existing rap renditions are overtly critical of American capitalism or militarism. At the same time, it is worth noting the centrality of the rap form to *Hamilton* and its updating of both the American immigrant experience and American musical theater.

For music to unite and shape us, it must be sufficiently open and inclusive to speak to the diverse members of contemporary communities. As our communities change and the traditions on which "we" draw multiply, so must our music develop. Then too, the best music will reflect the multiple values that Confucians seek to inculcate in us—the virtues that I will continue to discuss over the course of this book. Confucians have always seen violence and warfare as at least partial failures: possibly necessary and justified under some conditions, but always reflecting a deep imbalance in the world. This is why Kongzi declared that the music of King Wu was "perfectly beautiful but not perfectly good." We might say the same thing about another famous "Banner" performance, Whitney Houston's powerful rendition at the 1991 Super Bowl, just after the beginning of the first Gulf War. The orchestra's martial accompaniment, the many images of uniformed members of the military, and the fly-over by F-16s that followed all reinforce the conflation between patriotism and militarism, even jingoism; there is no room for nuance or thought of distant suffering. Contrast this with Hendrix. To my mind, at least, his Woodstock performance of the anthem does exactly what a modern Confucian should expect our best music to do: unite us across diversity, drawing on (and creating anew) traditions while reinforcing the multiple values that are at stake—and even, in this case, reminding us that it can be difficult to hold them all together at once. Confucians want us to face up to complexity and seek to change things for the better. So did Jimi Hendrix, with a version of "Banner" that deserves to be called "perfectly beautiful and perfectly good," and so can we as we reflect on and engage with the world.

8 | REFLECT REGULARLY

Prior to reading this book, which of the following figures would you have most strongly connected to "Chinese philosophy"?

1. An activist urging a selfish political leader to reform his ways
2. A solitary figure meditating
3. A general seeking to pacify an unsettled region
4. A teacher debating the meaning of classic texts with his students

I guess that many people would choose answer 2, but that is probably the least apt of all four options, at least for Confucianism. Mengzi was an activist who repeatedly met with rulers (and the same is true of many other Confucians); one of Wang Yangming's prominent roles was as a general, and his experiences both informed and were informed by his Confucian teachings;[1] Zhu Xi (and many other Confucians) was a famed teacher whose extensive conversations with students were recorded for posterity.

As for the solitary meditating figure, that is probably a Daoist or a Buddhist: schools of thought that are less grounded in concrete relationships with others, and indeed call for us to find emptiness or "non-self." Still, Confucians do put considerable emphasis on practices of reflection, including something called "quiet sitting." Let's explore what these practices were, why Confucians advocated them, and how to do them.

* * *

We can begin with the most straight-forward example of reflection in the *Analects*. Zengzi, one of Kongzi's senior students, reports:

> Every day I examine myself on three points. In my dealings with others, have I failed to do my best? In my interactions with friends, have I failed to be trustworthy? Finally, have I failed to practice the instructions of my teacher?[2]

The same word "examine" is used three other times in the *Analects*; in each case, the idea is similar: one looks within oneself and backwards in time.[3] The question is not so much the actions that one has taken but rather the motivations that underlay those actions. Zengzi casts his internal gaze back and asks whether his motivations throughout the day have lived up to the standards that he has set . . . or were there moments in which he let himself down, perhaps allowing himself to get away with doing less than his all?

The idea of returning to oneself, looking back and within, also comes up in the following passage from *Mengzi*. Morally mature people, Mengzi says, have trained themselves to be charitable to others. Thus:

> Suppose someone treats one in an outrageous manner. Faced with this, an exemplary person will look within [literally, return to oneself], saying "I must be lacking in humaneness and propriety, or else how could such a thing happen to me?" When, looking within oneself, one finds they have been humane and proper, and yet this outrageous treatment continues, then the exemplary person will look within, saying, "I must have failed to do my best for them." When, on looking within oneself, one finds they have done their best and yet this outrageous treatment continues, then the exemplary person will say, "This person does not know what they are doing. Such a person is no different from an animal. One cannot expect an animal to know better."[4]

Mengzi's idea that we should learn not to immediately blame others, but instead begin by "looking within" is fascinating in its own right, especially in light of modern psychological findings that individuals are generally much quicker to blame others than themselves when things go wrong.[5] As for the "looking within" itself, this is again a process of inner inspection of one's motives and the way they may have been manifested in action. Did you experience some sort of discomfort or lack of attention that led to, if not an inappropriate action, then perhaps a facial expression or other "microaggression" that helped to generate the other's problematic response?[6]

One point of looking within, in short, can be to help discover internal inconsistencies. We may be unintentionally undermining our overt goals or commitments; in other words, we can discover that there are ways in which we are divided against ourselves. This is why these reflections are framed negatively—"Have I failed to be trustworthy?"—rather than being positive dwellings on one's successes. Confucians' most general term for internal division is "selfishness." Selfishness is cutting oneself (or those close to one) off from more distant others. We are selfish to the extent that we think only of our own needs, our own perspectives, our own experiences. This is not to say that those close to us should not matter more to us than distant strangers—filial piety, after all, is based on the special bond one has with parents—but distance or difference should not equate to a lack of concern.

I have said that when we discover selfishness within, we find ourselves to be divided. How can Confucians be sure of this? Might one not be wholly, consistently selfish? No. Remember the idea of "sprouts"? All people have at least nascent, non-selfish impulses, so the other main function of reflection is to help us see and be guided by our non-selfish impulses toward a more balanced self. As we saw when exploring the idea of sprouts, "cultivation" is doing sustained work on ourselves in order most fully to realize the moral potential that is hinted at by our sprouts. Ultimately, if sustained cultivation is guided properly by reflection, Confucians believe that it is possible to have a unified, harmonious, balanced self.

Wang Yangming famously makes the case against pure selfishness, arguing that even a "petty person" will spontaneously feel alarm and commiseration upon suddenly seeing others in danger. (In fact, on Wang's telling, these "others" include non-human animals, plants, and even inanimate objects, which I will return to in Chapter 13.) As Wang puts it, "Although the heartmind of the petty person is divided and narrow, yet their humaneness which forms one body with all things can remain free from darkness to this degree."[7] There is an important difference between Wang and Mengzi—Wang thinks that humaneness is in a sense already complete within us but typically obscured, while Mengzi thinks that the nascent, positive potential within us needs to be grown in order to attain full-fledged humaneness—but we should not allow this difference to distract from their agreement on two key points. First, paying careful attention to our reactions can give us glimpses of the pure, non-selfish emotions of which we are capable; and second, selfishness is a continual challenge that we need to work to overcome.

So far, I have described reflection as an inward "examination"; that is, a looking within that allows us to notice non-selfish as well as selfish reactions. In two ways, reflection involves more than just "noticing." First, reflection is not merely cognitive. Just as musical harmony is naturally resonant and attractive, so too are harmonies within us—and disharmonies feel correspondingly "off" and un-welcome. Admittedly, we can usually repress or distract ourselves from internal inconsistencies, but insofar as we pay attention via reflection, we have a kind of emotional engagement with our-selves. This is an important aspect of the verb *si*, which in general we can translate as "to reflect." As the contemporary scholar Bryan Van Norden emphasizes, in some contexts it is quite explicit that to "*si*" something is to long for it, as in an ancient ode describing a gentleman as "longing for" his bride-to-be. After considering some other evidence, Van Norden concludes that to *si* (i.e., reflect on) the sprouts is "to focus one's attention on the sprouts in a way that involves longing for their proper development."[8] So reflecting (or *si*-ing, if you will) is clearly more than just thinking.

Second, reflection is not just a passive process. It is crucial that we can choose to reflect, choose where to direct our attention, and even move our attention from one situation to another and thus reflect on their relationship. This is in contrast to the way that our sensory organs work, which is to be passively drawn toward their objects. As we read in *Mengzi*:

> It is not the function of the ears and eyes to reflect, and they are misled by things. Things interact with things and simply lead them along. But the function of the heartmind is to reflect. If it reflects then it will attain [virtue].[9]

I will say more about the relation between reflection and virtue in a moment, but for now let us dwell on the implications of the heartmind's ability to initiate reflection. We can—as in Mengzi's famous thought experiment—ask how we would respond to suddenly seeing a baby about to fall into a well, or we can reflect back on actual experiences. Maybe you recently encountered a panhandler on a city street and then turned away, walking on without a word. Does reflection reveal some inner turmoil around this event? Mengzi would encourage each of us to employ reflection to seek to "extend" those reactions about which we feel good to other circumstances about which we are less proud of how we responded. It's easy to feel compassion for a baby, and probably to seek to save him or her from falling into the well—especially when all of this is in your imagination. When you're in a hurry, maybe frustrated about something at home or at work, it's harder to treat the panhandler like a person in need. Confucian writings about extension aim to help us see-and-feel the similarities in these situations, and thus ultimately to help us treat them the same.

The details of how one does this "extension" are debated by Confucians throughout the tradition, often specifically tied to how one engages in "sympathetic understanding." Sympathetic understanding is to use one's own reactions to understand and empathize with the situation of another, often by imagining oneself in their circumstances. At one point in the *Analects*, sympathetic understanding is glossed as "Do not impose on others what you yourself do not desire"—a formulation often called the "negative golden rule."[10] It would be a mistake, though, to think that extension and sympathetic understanding are simply about applying this rule. The rule helps learners to comprehend how you might "use yourself as an analogy" to feel appropriately toward another, which a related passage calls the "method of humaneness."[11] If you're vacillating on whether to reach out and try to help someone who's clearly struggling, imagining yourself in their shoes is a good starting place.

So, is reflection the whole answer to the challenge of being a good person? No, for two distinct reasons. First, at least for the mainstream Confucians that we've been focusing on, reflection on its own can be misleading. Already in the *Analects*, Kongzi is recorded as saying, "Study without reflection is a waste. Reflection without study is a danger."[12] Study without reflection is a waste because the real point of learning is self-development (and not just learning to spout facts or quote classical passages), and this cannot occur without reflecting on how what one reads is relevant to oneself and one's present context. This is precisely the lesson of Zhu Xi's approach to reading. Reflection without study, on the other hand, gambles one's development on one's own un-aided insight, rather than using a balanced approach that allows one to build on the insights of texts and teachers. Over the course of the long Confucian tradition there have been many different approaches to the balance of reflection and study; especially in times when the common practice has seemed weighed down by scholasticism or rhetorical excess, some thinkers have approached a pure reliance on reflection (on which a bit more in a moment).

The other reason why reflection is not sufficient is that the goal of Confucian teachings is not that we make paused, reflective, or forced reactions to circumstances we encounter—even if these reactions are correct—but rather that we respond to any situation with fluid, virtuous spontaneity. For all of us who fall short of sagehood—which is to say, myself and probably all my readers!—we will have to continue to engage in reflection. Reflection is not an end in itself, but part of a process of development. The *Mengzi* states:

> All things are complete in oneself. There is no greater joy than to look within and find oneself to be sincere. Nothing gets one closer to humaneness than forcing oneself to act out of sympathetic understanding.[13]

Forced sympathetic understanding is a good start.[14] Achieving sagehood is something we do by degrees, and at least sometimes we each can look within and experience the joy that Mengzi describes here. It is joyous to find that things fit together and make sense, that one is genuinely interested in one's work and cares about the outcomes, that one's friendships are real and sustaining, that one's loved ones are living good lives, and so on. To have "all things" fit together is a tall order—although as we'll see, apt negative emotions like grief or worry can be compatible with the special kind of "joy" that Mengzi is here describing. For now, the main point is to recognize that simply using one's reason to figure things out is a long way from the goal of Confucian cultivation.

* * *

Critical readers might be wondering if there are any downsides to pursuing a reflective way of life. Does it assume an unrealistic degree of transparency? Does it overly downplay the role of reason? Does it make sufficient room for social criticism? Responding to these challenges, I think, can lead to productive developments in the contemporary Confucian understanding of reflection.

If Freud is right, it is a mistake to believe that we can consciously understand our motivations. All too often, we lack access to the drives that actually control us. Wouldn't reflection that aims at finding guidance and unity be equally mistaken, resting on an illusion of transparent motives? A Confucian response to this challenge comes in three steps. First, it is true that if Freud is largely right about the specifics of our psyches, then Confucians are not. As Lee Yearley has put it, Confucians offer an invitation to view the self in a way quite different from Freud.[15] But, second, most of the various Confucian models of self do not rely on a naïve kind of transparency. It is easier to see (and be disturbed by) disunity than it is to see (and be confidently led by) unity; selfishness is always a concern and a potential source of distortion. Therefore, third, even though it is still early days in terms of Confucian theorists working with modern psychologists, there are some very promising ways in which non-Freudian psychological models line up with Confucian expectations, and vice versa.[16]

The second challenge I want to consider is whether the Confucian account of reflection gives too little room to pure reasoning. In ancient Greece, Aristotle argued that the life of contemplation—the pure, philosophical life—was the best way to live. Both Plato and Aristotle viewed knowledge and reason as distinct from and superior to feelings, and lauded reasoned choices over automatic (or spontaneous) reactions. These same observations apply to many subsequent giants in this development of Western philosophy. Confucian reflection, in contrast, is always understood as part of a process of improvement rather than an end in itself. Feeling is tied together with thinking, and reflection encompasses both. Confucians aim at the state of sagely ease, in which one responds spontaneously to situations without needing to reason or consciously choose, even if pausing and reflecting is sometimes needed for all of us who still fall short of sagehood. What, then, of the activity of philosophizing itself? Overall, Confucians see philosophy as continuous with the sorts of reflection on classical texts that are important parts of personal development for all people. Confucian theoretical writings are often framed as either formal commentaries on existing texts or more loosely organized reading notes; in each case, the theorist reflects on how various ideas and experiences fit together. Sometimes the resulting scholarship or theorizing is more novel; sometimes it is quite conventional. But in all cases part of the point is the activity of reflection itself—that is, the theorist's own, on-going process of personal development. In short, while it is true that explicit use of reason plays somewhat different roles in Confucian than in mainstream Greek thought, the Confucian approach to reason is nuanced and coherent, and it is far from clear that the Confucian approach is mistaken.

A final challenge concerns whether Confucian reflection is able to be sufficiently critical to motivate needed social and institutional changes. If reflection is aimed within, won't it miss seeing ways in which social, economic, and political structures systematically disadvantage or even oppress some people? In response, Confucians can point out that their ideal is one in which all perspectives are taken seriously and, to the extent that some perspectives may be dismissed or undervalued, this is an important failure of the kind of "unity" that reflection seeks. Some sorts of reflection can specifically aim at trying to uncover ways in which one's disconnection from others is hidden from oneself; recall here Mengzi's insistence that we look within—and even look again—when confronted with outrageous behavior. We will also see explicit discussion of the ways in which we should attend to our world broadly and inclusively in the next chapter. Still, to the extent that the oppression of others has not penetrated our awareness, reflection will be of limited help; this is especially true when institutional arrangements (like gated residential communities) seal us off from the experiences of others. Reflection cannot solve these problems on its own. As we'll explore more fully later on, institutional change and political action are needed as well.

Recall my suggestion that "a solitary figure meditating" is not a likely description of a Confucian. Classical Confucian texts say a good deal about the importance of reflection, as we have seen, but do not stipulate any particular way in which it must be done. Kongzi presumably did not envision people reflecting while jogging—which is my favorite time for extended reflection—but jogging is not so different from the solitary walks in nature that many later Confucians describe.[17] A regular morning or evening practice of reflection also fits well with Confucian prescriptions. And then there is "quiet sitting." Prior to the rise of Buddhism in China, this is a sparsely used term that just meant to sit quietly. During the first millennium CE, Buddhists appropriate the term as one way of talking about their formal practices of meditation. By around 1000 CE, scholars and practitioners of Neo-Confucianism begin to explicitly advocate "quiet sitting." Many leading Neo-Confucians take pains to emphasize that quiet sitting is not Buddhist meditation and even reject the idea that there is any specific way to practice it. Far from the Buddhist aim of cutting off thought and stilling one's heartmind, a typical Confucian attitude was Zhu Xi's: he aimed to find some tranquility before reading, for example, or when he was too sick or his eyes too strained to read, but says to avoid the kind of "unreflective" quiet sitting employed by Buddhists.[18] Some went further, seeking a kind of direct and pure insight; but for Zhu and other mainstream Confucians, this was dangerously subjectivist.[19]

Confucian reflection is something that all of us can readily undertake.[20] Maybe you're like me and you engage in it while running, or during another activity like cooking, or maybe you can just sit quietly and let your heartmind be still. A modest ritual to signal that you're entering a different, "quiet" mode will help. Look within, think back, savor moments of harmony and note any awkward internal divisions. Because reflection always comes after we've acted (or failed to act), it cannot be the whole answer to living a good Confucian life, but it is a crucial part of self-cultivation.

9 | PAY ATTENTION

There was plenty of room as I stepped onto the train. I put in my earbuds and got to work as the train trundled off. Sometime later I happened to look up and was surprised to see how crowded the car was becoming. An older man scanned for a place and then shuffled on, followed by a nervous-looking teenager on her own. I indignantly noted the way that veteran commuters around me were hoarding seats and avoiding eye contact . . . until I realized that my briefcase occupied an aisle seat next to me, and I was just as culpable! I hurriedly jammed my bag between my feet and tried to look welcoming, but the moment had passed.

As moral failings go, distractedly inconveniencing others may not seem like much. Even those who consciously look away or feign sleep are unlikely to be numbered among the worst sinners. According to Zhu Xi, though, the failure to cultivate the right skills of attention actually goes a long way toward explaining why his world so consistently fell short of the happy, harmonious community that it could be. He no doubt would say the same about our world in which marketing dollars and impenetrable algorithms combine to shape so much of what we see and want.

The importance of attention connects to other key Confucian ideas we have already seen. Being filial is partly about paying attention to your parents' needs and desires. We can only follow rituals if we pay attention to their (sometimes counter-intuitive) rules, and one of the points of rituals is to enable participants to notice things that one might otherwise miss. In other words, paying attention to rituals helps us pay attention to the emotions of self and others. We've also discussed paying attention to our emotional "sprouts," using periodic reflection to attend to our motivations, and so on. Why is attention at the heart of so many Confucian teachings?

* * *

Confucians tell us that we should focus on things over which we have some significant control. As we continue to explore Confucianism as a way of life, we'll have several opportunities to explore the Confucian attitude toward "fate," which is their term for everything outside of our control. For now, focus on one important idea: we have at best indirect and partial control over the results of our actions, but we can work on how we are poised to react to the situations we encounter.[1] Let me say that again, because it lies at the heart of so much Confucian thinking: we can do little to influence the results of our actions once we've made them, but we can at least partly shape how we're likely to react in the first place. If we can get ourselves to attend—perhaps by expending psychic resources, as in English the term "pay attention" implies— then we should notice and give due weight to relevant factors and be more likely to respond appropriately. Mengzi puts the point in memorable fashion, saying that we "should always be actively attending rather than forcing a correct outcome; neither forget our heartminds nor 'help them grow.'" He is referring to a foolish farmer who impatiently "helped his plants to grow"—that is, he pulled at the sprouts in an effort to make them grow faster—which of course killed the plants.[2] Active attention, then, is neither forcing nor ignoring. A central point of what Zhu Xi calls "reverential attention," in fact, is how it enables us to actively attend without paying a continuous psychic cost.

A good (patient, attentive) reaction does not guarantee a good outcome. Sometimes the odds are stacked against you. But a bad outcome also becomes a further situation to which you can react; our ethical lives go on. At any rate, our question concerns the role of attention in all of this. An initial answer is that the Confucians stress attention because it both strongly influences our reactions and because it is sufficiently under our control. My own experience on the crowded train should be enough to demonstrate that attention influences our reactions in at least one way: because I was not paying attention, I did not react at all until it was too late! But then again, it's not that I wasn't paying attention to anything: in fact, I was focused quite intensively on my laptop. Clearly, we need to learn more about what kind of attention is needed and how it can be developed.

Confucians would say that the very narrow attention that I was paying to my laptop was a kind of selfishness, and it is hard not to agree. I was blocking a seat that others needed, just so I could be a little less cramped. It is obvious that my mild convenience shouldn't outweigh the needs and rights of others to a seat. Of course I wasn't doing this on purpose, but my decision to take two seats and then tune out from my environment clearly had a bad effect. Let's call this "selfish attention": when what one is attending to (what is mattering most to one at a given moment) isn't actually the thing that should be mattering most to one at that moment. At the other extreme, we can imagine someone whose attention wanders so much—always looking around, people watching, taking in the scenery—that nothing gets done. Because you may say that just passing the time while waiting in line for coffee is fine, here is a slightly different example of attention wandering. Imagine a sixteen-year-old high-school student being asked to read in a history book about ideal relationships between political authorities and their advisers. How easy would it be for him to get distracted by a detail that reminds him of some drama in his own life? Add in instant messaging and his social media fix, and hours may pass without much progress on the history book. This, too, is a kind of selfishness (call it "selfish wandering"), with attention flitting from one aspect of his personal world to another without leaving room for tomorrow's history class, much less the exemplary advisers of a 16th-century monarch.

Zhu Xi's idea of reverential attention is meant to avoid both kinds of selfishness. To some readers "reverence" may sound like an attitude that only belongs in church. It is true that formal religious ceremonies seek to evoke reverence, but it is a much broader notion. Zhu felt that poetry could be particularly effective at pointing toward what we are supposed to revere. One of his philosophical heroes wrote:

Near midday the clouds are light and the wind gentle.
Standing by the flowers and following the willow, I look across the river.
Bystanders do not understand the joy of my heart.
They will say that I seek to be lazy like young people.[3]

Zhu believes that a fundamentally positive orientation to life is manifested, to at least some degree, in everyone. We can see this in the ways that we care for one another, including strangers and even other aspects of our shared world so long as we notice them. The mutual dependence and mutual concern that are easiest to see within the intimate relationships of a family in fact pervade the cosmos, Zhu says. Zhu's cosmos has no creator or deity; each of us is a part of the cosmos, each a co-creator of each new day. Just look, he says, and you will see. Or rather, once you start to attend to the ways in which we together create the living cosmos, you will feel (as well as see) the interconnections. This feeling—the awe and joy sparked by feeling one's place among fellow humans as well as meandering clouds, gently swaying flowers, and flowing river—lies at the heart of reverence.

The phrase "feeling one's place among" is particularly important in that last sentence. Reverence is not an experience of un-differentiated oneness, but of things fitting together, even if many of these interconnections are beyond one's ability to perceive or even grasp (which helps to explain why "awe" is one dimension of reverence: the cosmos is vast[4]). The idea of reverential attention is therefore that one is attuned to the broad significance of any situation one encounters: how particular details relate to others, what matters most, and so on. In Zhu's own terms, a heartmind that is rev-erentially attentive has a "master." For some contemporary readers the word "master" may be immediately connected to slavery and the idea that one human can treat another as a thing, something to be owned and completely controlled. What Zhu has in mind is crucially different, more like the head of a family, even if this is still more hierarchical than many contemporary conceptions. As a later Neo-Confucian explains it, the heartmind's having a master is like when the master of the house is at home. When the master is at home things are naturally in order and chaotic outsiders are prevented from entering the house—even without the master's actively warding them away. Similarly, when one is attuned to the broad significance of any given affair, then "chaos"—that is, selfish concerns—cannot enter one's heartmind.[5]

Reverential attention, then, means to attend to all that one encounters in daily life and to do so from a stance of reverence for interconnected life. We all know people who pay careful attention to their surroundings, but for some reason do so in order to seek out flaws, to nitpick, to undermine. To pay reverential attention is instead to notice and look to reinforce care for life, care for others, and care for the self. We can think of this as looking for harmony.[6] This does not mean that one is actively steering what one sees. Rather, one is looking for harmony in the sense that one is primed to see and react favorably to opportunities for harmony—ways that things fit together well—because even as one is attending single-mindedly to a particular person or thing, in all their distinctness, this will simultaneously include being aware of their interdependence with the entire context. Skilled managers of any kind of team do this all the time, taking seriously their interactions with each team member while simultaneously noting possible ways in which members can work together even better. Perhaps there's a way to adjust roles so that each finds their responsibilities even more satisfying, or perhaps there's some misunderstanding the manager notices that, when cleared up, will help colleagues work together more fluidly. One way to think about the ubiquitous relevance of reverential attention, then, would be to think of the entire cosmos as all part of one team—and we each have opportunities to be its manager.

Zhu Xi's prolific writings lay out many ways in which one can do this. He writes about how one should carry oneself, dress, behave in public and at home: all these things influence when and how one can be attentive. As you'll remember, Zhu also writes about how one should study: the ancient classics are great sources of inspiration, but only if one reads deeply rather than shallowly, always looking for ways in which the experiences described in the texts relate to one's own world and own life, today. Zhu believes that this kind of studying can gradually alter one's dispositions, which is to say that as one learns to see oneself in other situations, or to imagine others in one's own shoes, one's tendencies and temperament change.

* * *

Perhaps reverential attention sounds like permanent, naïve optimism. In one sense this is true. Zhu believes that a reverent sense of awe for the interconnected life thrumming throughout the cosmos can be powerful enough to keep us oriented toward it, even in the face of great trials. But this does not mean to be naïvely unaware of suffering. Awareness of and concern for suffering is a central part of the care for one-and-all that reverential attention enables. In addition, when one notices a problem from a standpoint of reverential attention, one's orientation toward interconnected life helps to direct one's emotional and behavioral reactions in fruitful directions, rather than leaving one despondent. Not long ago, my country was rocked by the twin challenges of the COVID-19 pandemic and rage at police brutality against Black people (in the aftermath of the murder of George Floyd, Breonna Taylor, and others). All this was further exacerbated by the extreme self-obsession of a president who viewed everything through the sole lens of its relation to his hold on power—to the extent that obviously prudent steps to protect others, like wearing a mask in public, somehow became political statements and were thus resisted by the president's hardcore supporters. It would have been easy to despair.

Reverential attention is the stance of viewing what is before one through the lens of concern for interconnected life: this is what matters most and what should shape our attention. Thinking back to the summer of 2020 when I first drafted this chapter, what that meant to me was to be aware of and inspired by the leadership being demonstrated by Black Americans, and to do my best to learn from them. It meant to be aware of and inspired by my colleagues' activism. It meant to be aware of and inspired by my daughters' drives to improve their societies, one as a scientist working to discover new medicines and the other as a field organizer working to elect progressive candidates. Shaped by these realities, my emotional and behavioral reactions to horrible, national events and even to minor, local setbacks could be hopeful and positive—and in no way merely naïve. As I'll emphasize shortly, these hopeful and positive reactions should furthermore result in active engagement with one's world.

Failing to develop reverential attention can lead to despair, but it can also lead to a kind of selfish detachment that the great novelist and philosopher Iris Murdoch calls "fantasy." She writes:

> The chief enemy of excellence in morality (and also in art) is personal fantasy: the tissue of self-aggrandizing and consoling

wishes and dreams which prevents one from seeing what is there outside one. . . . We see in mediocre art, where perhaps it is even more clearly seen than in mediocre conduct, the intrusion of fantasy, the assertion of the self, the dimming of any reflection of the real world.[7]

Fantasy, for Murdoch, is a construal of our situation that is "consoling": we find a way to see our situation according to which nothing is our fault, we have no responsibilities, and we can pursue our hopes and pleasures as we see fit. This is nothing like reverential attention, which calls for us to pay engaged attention to our actual situations, in all their interconnected complexity. Fantasy, on the other hand, thrives on disconnection; it flourishes in environments like gated communities, in which inhabitants purposely cut themselves off from their surrounding communities.

A second concern about reverential attention is that it might be too hard to do, or at least impossible to sustain. Recall that earlier in the chapter I acknowledged the cost implied by our phrase "paying attention." Cognitive scientists have emphasized that this is more than mere metaphor: cognitive control is a "limited resource" and sustained efforts at focus can deplete it. One scholar notes that it is possible to succeed in attending in one domain or for a time, but paying attention can exhaust us, ultimately undermining our motivation (think of the "Zoom fatigue" many experienced during the COVID-19 pandemic).[8] The kind of attention for which Zhu Xi is calling, however, is different from forced, controlled focus. Instead, being able to engage in reverential attention is closer to what another group of cognitive scientists has called being a "moral chronic." Such people have "chronically accessible moral schemas

[that] dispose [them] to 'see' readily the moral dimensions of experience."[9] The details are complicated (and not at all settled), but the core idea is that particular "schemas" or "frames" can deploy more or less automatically, and when one's psychological development has taken place in the right ways, these "chronic" reactions can lead one to interpret the world in moral terms. Scientists have pointed out that this matches well with the fact that morally impressive people who have been studied by sociologists often report that they experience taking a moral action not as a voluntary choice but as necessary—that is, they see the moral course of action as obvious rather than as one among other alternatives.[10] Relying on rituals and other techniques I have been discussing, we cultivate ourselves so that a virtuous orientation like reverential attention becomes increasingly automatic and authentic. To the extent we succeed, "looking for harmony" will not be taxing; instead, one will spontaneously employ ways of seeing that highlight possibilities for harmony.

Even if Zhu Xi is right that we all have a fundamentally positive orientation to life and that the right kind of cultivation can help us make this into a widely applicable, ingrained way of seeing, it still may seem that individuals with high levels of reverential attention will be rare. Where does this leave the rest of us? Here it is worth connecting the Confucians' emphasis on things like ritual and dress with the observations that many contemporary critics have made about the "attention economy." We are coming to better understand the ways in which technology companies—drawing on cognitive science research—have been designing our computers and especially our cell phones to monopolize an ever-greater share of our attention (and thus potential income from advertisers).

The best responses are not those that just call on us to ignore the siren call of apps (or to abandon technology altogether) but those emphasizing that we should design our technology to support the ways that we want to live. A good phone interface, just like a good outfit or good greeting ritual, makes it easier to attend to what really matters and harder to get caught in endless cycles of distraction.[11]

Maybe endless cycles of distraction do not sound all that appealing, but a final concern we should consider is whether reverential attention is too serious: Maybe we need to loosen up and allow for at least some distraction? After all, one of Zhu Xi's sources when it came to the idea of reverential attention, the philosopher Cheng Yi, had the reputation of being a rigid taskmaster with little sense of humor.[12] We live in such stressful times: Surely we deserve a break?

The issue of humor is a red herring. There is no connection between having reverence for a life-filled, interdependent cosmos and lacking a funny bone. As Paul Woodruff says in his wonderful book on reverence, "Reverence and a keen eye for the ridiculous are allies: both keep people from being pompous or stuck up."[13] The question of how much and what kind of distraction we should allow for, though, is well worth our time. Recall from the beginning of the chapter that we're looking for an attitude that is neither "selfish attention" nor "selfish wandering." It seems to me that when cultural critics speak on behalf of drift and distraction, their assumption is usually that we have only two choices: carefully planned, deliberate "attention," or else distracted, playful wandering.[14] But reverential attention is neither of these. Instead of a narrow focus that shuts out the rest of the interdependent world— as I did when I sat down on the train—reverential attention means to always keep the context in view, shifting attention as needed. Tasks that need extended, uninterrupted attention are only compatible with true reverential attention insofar as one prepares a context in which such narrow focus can be appropriately sustained. As for how one can prepare such a context: ultimately this is going to depend on working with other people, in one's family or in one's society.

10 | BE ENGAGED

Feminists from the 1970s to the present have insisted that "the personal is political." Confucians for many centuries have invoked the phrase "inner sage, outer king." These two slogans share an insight but also have room to learn from one another. The feminist slogan is mainly about making the personal more political: that is, emphasizing that so-called personal matters like the relation between spouses within a family are shaped by broad social structures, and thus genuine, lasting changes in "personal" relations require "political" movements. The Confucian slogan, in contrast, is mainly about making the political more personal, in the sense that one's ability and motivation to act well in the "political" realm is tied to one's "personal" development, and so anyone who cares about political improvements should attend to their personal cultivation.

There is another important side to the Confucian slogan. Acting as an "outer king" is not a simple outcome of being an "inner sage": rather, "outer" action is a necessary part of the process of "inner" development. In other words, one does not first fully develop on the "inside," and only at the end have this inner development manifest "outside." I'll explain this further in a moment, but for now it's useful to see how there is still a contrast with feminism. Feminists think that only when "political" action has resulted in dramatic changes to socio-political structures will it reliably be possible to live just and equitable "personal" lives. Confucians, on the other hand, have historically tended to imply that while "political" action is required for "personal" development, successful changes to socio-political structures are not similarly required for one to be a good person and live a good life.

I have been putting "personal" and "political" in quotes so far to signal that—at least insofar as they apply to Confucians—they might not have exactly the same meanings that feminists tend to assign to them. The scope of the engagement that Confucians call on us to undertake is broad and varied, some of it overtly political but some not. Furthermore, Confucians believe that inner development and external engagement are intimately linked, an idea that feminists and other contemporary social critics should take seriously.

* * *

To flesh out the meaning of "inner sage, outer king" according to the Confucian tradition, it will suffice to look at two passages. The first comes from a short, classical-era text called *Greater Learning*. Near its beginning are a few lines that became almost a catechism for later Confucians:

Wanting to light up the bright virtue of all in the world, the ancients first put their states in order. Those who wanted to put their states in order first regulated their families. Those who wanted to regulate their families first cultivated their selves. Those who wanted to cultivate their selves first rectified their heartminds. Those who wanted to rectify their heartminds first made their intentions sincere. Those who wanted to make their intentions sincere first reached understanding. Reaching understanding lies in getting a handle on things.[1]

Exactly what Confucians of a given era meant by "rectifying their heartminds" or "getting a handle on things" is less important for our present purposes than the connection drawn between outer goals—the grandest of which was enabling all people to realize full virtue—and more local and, ultimately, inner goals.

Does this mean that the innermost steps literally need to come first, and thus that only someone who had completed the process of inner development (an "inner sage") could appropriately act in the wider world (an "outer king")? Or is the passage signaling a more flexible dependency between inner and outer? I join with the many Confucians who have read it in the latter way—and thus as not limiting engagement with the world to the morally perfect. Indeed, if full-fledged attainment of sagehood is something no one ever really achieves (which, spoiler alert, I do think!), then it makes much more sense to agree with those like the modern scholar Chen Xiyuan who writes: "We should see moral cultivation as requiring actualization in terms of the socio-political order at each stage and level of political engagement."[2]

A powerful reason for seeing inner development and outer expression as linked at every stage comes from Wang Yangming's famous insistence on the "unity of knowledge and action." Drawing explicitly on the same text I just discussed, the *Greater Learning*, Wang writes that:

> Genuine knowledge and action are [unified in the same way as when we] love beautiful colors. Seeing beautiful colors corresponds to knowledge, while loving beautiful colors corresponds to action. However, as soon as one sees that beautiful color, one has already, automatically loved it. It is not that one sees it first and them makes up one's mind to love it.[3]

Wang calls any knowledge that falls short of activating emotions and action "shallow": truly knowing something means that a response must follow automatically. One cannot be said to have attained real inner moral growth unless it makes us act accordingly, at least to some degree. Admittedly, the mere fact that one does something should not be taken as a guarantee of genuine knowledge because one might be doing it for the wrong, selfish reason; but one cannot claim moral progress unless one is simultaneously striving to put one's knowledge into action. In other words, the processes of "cultivating the self" through "making intentions sincere," "reaching understanding," and so on must necessarily be tied to doing things like "regulating a family" or "putting a state in order," depending on one's particular context.

Let's pause here for a moment to ask a couple questions: Are these claims that genuine inner development must issue in outer action convincing? Does this give us further reason to engage in social action, or is the lesson just that we should cultivate ourselves internally and hope that outer action follows? In response to the first question, ask yourself this: what would you make of someone who said "Yes, I am a filial child and care for my parents," but felt no concern for their well-being and took no steps to make their lives easier? This is bizarre even to think about, and certainly suggests deep failures of understanding and sincerity (and probably even deeper problems). Because the development that the Confucians advocate is precisely about how we see, feel, and react to the world's stimuli, the idea that we could make progress without it being manifest externally simply makes no sense.

As for the second question, it's actually rather misleading to think that we could do one without the other. Each of the chapters in this part of the book has discussed things that Confucians do in order to live a Confucian life, which is to say to grow as moral, virtuous people. Our nascent moral capacities fill out as we read about role models, interact with others, and reflect on how that goes. Outer action puts us in contexts that allow us to expand the perspectives we can draw upon, which in turn supports reverential attention: the ability to see what is before one in its interdependent context. So yes, it is true that one reason to be engaged in one's society is because it will help one continue to grow; this same insight can be seen behind the requirements at many American high schools that students do a certain amount of community service to graduate. But the more we grow the more we desire to better our world simply because we feel connected to it and care about it. Engagement makes us better, and the better we are, the more natural it is to engage.

Wang's "unity of knowledge and action" teaching was inspirational for activists from his own time down to the present, but it is important for us to understand that "engagement" need not always mean trying to overthrow a corrupt emperor or an illegitimate regime. Indeed, an oft-quoted passage from the *Analects* reads as follows:

> Someone said to Kongzi, Why are you not in government? The Master said, The *Documents* says, "Be ye filial, only filial, be friendly toward your brothers, and you will contribute to the government." This, too, is being in government.[4]

Kongzi draws on the ancient *Documents* to assert that filial and fraternal concern also contribute to achieving the aim of government, which we recall from the *Greater Learning* is to "light up the bright virtue of all in the world." There is a continuity, Kongzi is implying, between engaging with others in one's family and the more ambitious forms of engagement that we normally associate with being "in government."

From the standpoint of our larger and more complex contemporary societies it is possible to identify many forms of engagement, ranging from personal to public and from informal to formal, as suggested on this chart:

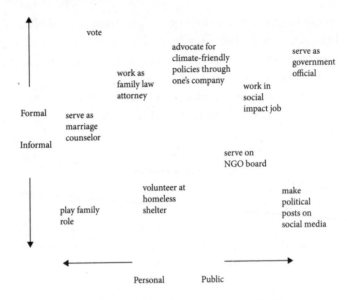

By formal, I mean activities that are associated with governing and/or professional roles, while informal refers to things that are more distant from laws and regulations or are volunteer based. The personal–public dimension is meant to capture the scope of the activity's participants or the magnitude of its intended impact. Voting is a personal activity (even though its ultimate outcome can be very broad), whereas serving as a volunteer board member at a social services non-profit is quite informal but is much more public than voting: one takes a visible stand by serving in a leadership role. If we return to the *Greater Learning*, we might sum up by saying that engagement is any sort of formal or informal activity aimed at impacting one's community for the better, where "better" is understood as orderly ("the ancients first put their states in order") and ultimately virtue-filled ("lighting up the bright virtue of all in the world").

* * *

There are many questions one could ask about engagement in this sense, the most obvious of which is: Must engagement always aim at "order"? What about activism that employs disorderly methods or even aims to disrupt current relations of power in deeper ways? Must Confucians eschew such forms of resistance?

To answer we need to begin with clearer definitions. Let's distinguish "engagement" as any activity aimed at impacting one's community for the better, from *Greater Learning*-engagement, which more narrowly specifies that "better" is understood in the manner I noted just above. "Engagement" can therefore cover both efforts that follow existing norms to improve things that these norms identify as problems, and efforts that reject existing norms as themselves problematic. These latter activities we can designate as "resistance," which a recent thinker has defined as "dissenting acts and practices, which [can] include lawful and unlawful acts, and expresses an opposition and refusal to conform to the established institutions and norms."[5] Resistance is one type of engagement—and at least on the surface its rejection of the existing "order" seems to make it incompatible with *Greater Learning*-engagement in one or both of two ways. On the one hand, one might resist the substance of a traditional order; on the other hand, one might carry out one's resistance in a "disorderly" (at least in terms of traditional norms) manner.

Even a cursory look at Confucian writings would reveal that they are often bitingly critical of some practices current in their day. Commenting on the ceremonies being performed by a noble he considers to be illegitimate, Kongzi lamented, "If this can be borne, what cannot be borne?"[6] Elsewhere Kongzi explicitly rejects a widely accepted change to earlier ritual practices.[7] These efforts to change the status quo can be squared with a goal of "order" only when we realize that not all forms of order are equally good. It is true that in both cases I just cited, Kongzi is implicitly calling for a return to older norms, but the lesson to take from this is not that he is a rigid traditionalist. Rather, Confucians seek an order that allows for the harmonious, non-coercive flourishing of all, and believe that such a society was actually realized in the early reigns of the Zhou dynasty rulers. This is not a book about Confucian political thought and so I cannot delve deeply into these matters, but perhaps it will suffice to note two things. First, the key question for Confucians has not been "Was the early Zhou dynasty actually harmonious?" but rather "What would allow for a society to be harmonious?" And second, the general answer to this latter question was this: societies are harmonious when virtuous rulers using non-coercive rituals enable the people to thrive, which leads to the people trusting the rulers and one another.[8] Admittedly, as noted at the outset of this chapter, Confucians have tended to do this in piecemeal fashion—critiquing one bad ritual or one bad person—rather than systemically. Therefore, they still have important things to learn from feminists about what "the personal is political" can mean.

Be this as it may, we can still conclude that Confucians may at times want to resist social norms and laws that stand in the way of their ideal society, and historically they sometimes did so. The remaining question is whether they can do so in a "disorderly" fashion. In general, the answer we find in Confucian texts is that we should do our best to strive to be orderly resisters. Within the family, recall, one is supposed to remonstrate "gently" when a parent errs. Ministers and others with a political voice are expected to try to "rectify" their ruler's heartmind, but to be governed by propriety as they do so. One of the most famous Confucian dissidents, Fang Xiaoru (1357–1402), refused to accept the legitimacy of the usurper when the emperor he had served was overthrown. Standing rather than kowtowing, Fang made a ritually proper (as addressed to a prince, not a new emperor) request for the whereabouts of the erstwhile emperor. The furious usurper had him and his family executed.

For most of us, orderly resistance may be too much to ask, at least some of the time. Resistance is difficult and none of us are sages, so perhaps we can be forgiven for outbursts of anger that may spill over onto undeserving targets or for rudeness occasioned by extreme frustration. Furthermore, the respect that we read into Fang Xiaoru's behavior may sometimes be unwarranted. Fang was presumably expressing respect not for the murderous usurper but for the institution and values of royalty, but what if those institutions and values are themselves the problem? More generally, should oppressed people be required to respectfully complain to their oppressors?

It might be that there are situations in which the existing norms are so thoroughly corrupt, and people so corrupted, that the only apt response is to "burn it down." Uncompromising revolution is deeply out of tune with central Confucian commitments, however. Peaceful protest and even civil disobedience—which is a ritualized form of political expression, calling attention to serious problems without rejecting the underlying system of laws and constitutionalism—fit better with Confucians' efforts to keep harmony in view. Still, seeking harmony does not mean docility; harmony does not teach us to sit back and take it unless we are able to respond in a perfect, measured way. Underreaction is at least as bad a fault as overreaction, and a modest overreaction is certainly better than a severe underreaction.[9] In sum, Confucian engagement can certainly encompass resistance, even sometimes unruly resistance.

Maybe we ought to ask: Isn't engagement sometimes too fraught or fruitless to be worth it? Shouldn't we sometimes withdraw? (And didn't Kongzi himself say so?) In the summer of 2020 as I originally drafted these words, it was easy to imagine citizens of Hong Kong asking precisely these questions. A year earlier huge protests energized the city-state, as much as a quarter of the entire population marched against a new law that further encroached on their autonomy from China and on their civil and legal rights. A year later, although that law had been withdrawn, China imposed a sweeping security law—bypassing Hong Kong's own legislative processes—while at the same time many democracy activists were arrested. In this context, the Confucian theorist and University of Hong Kong professor Joseph Chan published an op-ed in a local paper asking what Kongzi means when he says: "When the Way prevails, show yourself; when the Way is lost, conceal yourself."[10]

Drawing on the rest of the *Analects*, Chan shows that when Kongzi talks of "concealing" oneself, he means resigning from formal governmental roles and doing one's best to avoid physical danger—so that one can continue to struggle for what is right over the long haul.[11] "Concealing" does not mean withdrawing completely from society. As another contemporary scholar emphasizes,

"Although [one] may have no obligation, in certain cases, to take up government office, [one] does have an obligation to identify corruption in government as corruption, and [one] cannot fulfill this responsibility in complete isolation from others."[12] We humans must live in community, after all; beyond the needs for physical reproduction and mutual security, we find ourselves unavoidably caring for others, flourishing together. As Kongzi puts it when challenged by a recluse, "a person cannot flock together with the birds and the beasts."[13] The details of what sort of engagement makes the most sense will depend on one's capacities and context. If one is to grow as a person, though, the "political" (in the broad sense I have been using) must always be "personal."

Part Three

Making Progress

11 | COMMITMENT

Imagine that your son (or brother, or boyfriend) is struggling. He takes every minor setback personally and flares with anger at trifles; sometimes it seems that he is mad at the world. Then you hear from a friend of his that they had had a heart-to-heart about his stubbornness and irascibility, and your son for the first time had said he wanted to begin doing something to bring himself under control. How good that would feel! In the months and years since, your son has followed through in various ways: hanging inspirational posters on the walls of his room, reading stories about people who've worked through similar challenges, taking long walks during which he tries to work things through, and talking with friends and counselors. He has setbacks, but over time you feel like he's made progress: more empathic, less high-strung, more at peace. It all seems to have started with that heart-to-heart with his friend.

The story I've just sketched is one of making and trying to deepen (or live out) a commitment and is based on the life of the Ming dynasty Confucian Wu Yubi (1392–1469), who recorded his struggles and moral growth in a remarkable journal.[1] There are various stages through which we progress as we put Confucianism into practice, including making a commitment to become a better person. We'll look at others in turn, but this is a good place to begin. (Officially, one is supposed to aim at becoming a "sage." More on that later.) Commitments are interesting in their own right—why would it matter to say, "I will do something about my problems"?—but they also are valuable in the way they lead us to consider where the motivation to change comes from. Real commitments turn out not to be just one-off actions, but life-long undertakings.

* * *

Among the most famous passages in the *Analects* is the following, which has been described as Kongzi's spiritual autobiography:

> At fifteen, I committed myself to learning; at thirty, I took my place in society; at forty, I became free of doubts; at fifty, I understood Heaven's mandate; at sixty, my ear was attuned; and at seventy, I could follow my heartmind's desires without overstepping the bounds of propriety.[2]

For present purposes, the most important things about this statement are first, that it begins with a commitment (at age fifteen!); second, that a lengthy process of learning and growth ensues; and third, that by age seventy Kongzi has reached a point at which apt behavior comes naturally, smoothly, without internal struggle.

(Implicitly, then, prior to seventy things weren't so easy.) The word "commitment" only comes up once here, but in reality this whole passage is about coming to really *have* the commitment that adolescent Kongzi announces. Commitment, that is, can be superficial or deep. This is made clear in two other *Analects* passages. Compare:

> The Master said, If a scholar is committed to the Way, but is ashamed of having bad clothes or bad food, he is not worth taking counsel with.[3]

with

> The Master said, If once he is committed to humaneness, he will have no hatred.[4]

The first describes a shallow commitment that has not affected one's entire personality, whereas the latter is a mature commitment that influences one's emotions and judgments.[5]

The idea that commitments come in differing degrees is familiar to us today. New Year's resolutions apparently go back at least four thousand years to ancient Babylon; today, the most common month in which Americans purchase a new gym membership is January, as they try to put their resolutions into practice.[6] Sadly, according to one survey 63 percent of gym memberships go completely unused; another showed that exercise dropped off dramatically as early as the second Friday in January. Clearly, just having a good intention (and even putting money into it) is not enough to live up to a commitment.[7]

A fascinating perspective on commitments comes from Alcoholics Anonymous (AA), the decades-old fellowship of individuals dedicated to solving their drinking problems and to helping others do so as well. On the one hand, the Twelve Steps of AA do include explicit acknowledgments, such as:

1. We admitted we were powerless over alcohol—that our lives had become unmanageable.
3. Made a decision to turn our will and our lives over to the care of God as we understood Him.[8]

AA starts with recognizing and admitting a problem. On the other hand, "AAs never swear off alcohol for life, never take pledges committing themselves not to take a drink 'tomorrow.'"[9] They focus on not drinking now and leave tomorrow for the future. The one thing that they can rely on—and, generally, find that they continue to need—is the continued presence of a group of fellow alcoholics who are also committed to avoiding drinking each day. AAs share their stories together and also read the stories of others who have struggled with and yet managed to stop drinking: the "Big Book," *Alcoholics Anonymous*, was originally published in 1939 and contains more than forty such stories.[10]

Kongzi's fifteen-year-old "commitment to learning" was based on a desire to change himself, not to rid himself of drinking but to become more like the exemplary people he had heard about from the early Zhou dynasty. As the movement he helped to establish grew, it took on the features discussed so far in this book: an emphasis on moral growth through ritual, reading, and engagement, aimed at becoming less selfish and ultimately a sage. Mentors and teachers came to play more explicit roles, modelled in part on Kongzi's own relationship with his students. Rituals and fellowship functioned in some ways similarly to AA meetings in helping Confucian learners to continue on their path, but it is worth reiterating that Kongzi in the *Analects* is depicted as achieving a kind of transformation that AA does not contemplate. Kongzi at seventy has what later thinkers describe as a "mature commitment": a sincere, unified, integrated personality that manifests spontaneously, without the need for striving or control. It is intriguing to ask why this difference between Confucianism and AA might exist. One possibility is that it has to do with the status of alcoholism as a disease without a cure. More salient in AA literature, though, is the role of God (admittedly, subject to any interpretation) as different from oneself and as the only power that can help one. In contrast to this idea of turning to an outside "other" for help, Confucians conceptualize us as enlarging ourselves to be more connected to others, and in principle see no limits to this connectedness.

* * *

I'll circle back to these large ideas toward the end of the chapter, but for now let's notice that all the stages of commitment are closely bound up with the question of motivation. What motivates one to make an initial commitment, and what can keep one carrying on? How do people like Wu Yubi manage it? It's well and good to say that fellowship helps, but why? Analyzing what our various Confucian sources have said, I believe we can find four distinct sources of motivation, two that we can classify as "outer" (rituals/

traditions and other people, especially teachers) and two that are more "inner" (pushes and pulls).

More about these types of motivation in a moment, but it will be helpful first to note that none of them match up very well with the way that what contemporary economists call "commitments" motivate us. For the economists, to make a commitment is to do something that changes the costs or benefits of making some further decision. Putting down a non-refundable deposit toward a purchase makes it harder to back out, and so is a "commitment device."[11] Having a commitment in this sense just means that calculations of costs work out differently than if one didn't have the "commitment," whereas for Confucians, commitment is bound up with changes to one's motivational structure, personality, and worldview. According to Confucians, that is, "establishing a commitment" involves partly recognizing some value that one wants to align with more consistently and wholeheartedly. Think of the difference between committing to attend a certain college (by making a deposit) and committing to be an anti-racist (an ongoing process involving reading, reflection, and action). Kongzi's commitment to learning is obviously of the latter type.

Turning now to the sources of motivation that lead one to establishing and deepening a commitment, the first type is the rituals and traditions within which one grows up and lives their life. Children have little choice but to carry out the rituals demanded of them, and social norms keep pressure on adults as well, so the question of why we are motivated to undertake rituals largely answers itself. In addition, as we have seen, rituals contribute to our moral development and so help to nurture the more internal motivations I'll talk about soon. Of course, it is always possible to wonder why one should continue to follow a given ritual or honor some tradition; other chapters have both offered such reasons and allowed that critical engagement with existing traditions is part of keeping tradition vital.

Other people play an implicit role in what I have just said about rituals: as the source of sanctions for non-compliance and potentially as the targets of efforts to reason about changing rituals. But other people play another function as well, which can best be seen in considering the role of a teacher. All the great Confucians were teachers. Mengzi is a good example. His most important students were probably not those who formally acknowledged him as their teacher, but rather the political leaders for whom he served as mentor. I say "mentor" because he did much more than just offer policy advice. In one exchange that is recorded between Mengzi and the somewhat wayward King Xuan of Qi, the two move quickly from talking in general terms about what a "true king" is to a sort of therapy session in which Mengzi probes and uncovers the king's desires and deep motivations. At one point the king explicitly asks Mengzi to "aid my commitment."[12] How do teachers do this?

Zhu Xi says that the key to students' establishing their commitments is to "teach them to be courageous and fierce, after which they will naturally make progress."[13] He does this partly through abstract teaching about what humans are capable of and partly through encouraging his students to work hard—ever harder—at the practices of self-cultivation that he lays out. "Don't wait!" he exhorts them; you can do it, if you only try, so be bold![14] I called Mengzi a "mentor" a moment ago; perhaps "life coach" would also be appropriate for the role I am describing. Indeed, as the contemporary scholar Aaron Stalnaker has explored in detail, the role of the Confucian "Master" is in many ways like a teacher or coach helping one to cultivate a certain kind of performative skill.[15] Among other things, Confucian teaching is aimed at developing a "skilled attention" that allows one to do certain things effortlessly while focusing in on particularly difficult problems.

I have said that the internal motivations that fund our commitments come in two varieties, but I should clarify that I refer to the motivations of which we are conscious, or which we can articulate if questioned. Often, and increasingly as one grows within a Confucian program of moral development, one's reactions are spontaneous and motivations are unconscious. Kongzi at age seventy had no need for pausing and consulting his conscious motives. If he was asked why he did what he did, he might just say it was the obvious thing to do. Studies show that this is how many exemplary people describe their state of mind when making what seems from the outside to be a difficult, courageous decision (such as choosing to take in and hide a Jew during the Holocaust).[16] Nonetheless, Confucians (including the Master himself) regularly refer to two varieties of inner motive which I am calling "push" and "pull."[17]

"Push" motivations are the results of concerns about the present state of oneself and the world. Unease pushes one to change. According to the 20th-century Confucian Xu Fuguan, in fact, a "consciousness of concern" is the defining feature of Confucianism and lies behind Confucians' active engagement with the world.[18] Crucially, the target of Confucians' concern is not their own material success but their moral development and, ultimately, the harmony and flourishing of the wider world. In the

Analects, we read: "An exemplary person worries about the Way, not about personal poverty."[19] Mengzi expands on this:

> An exemplary person has life-long worries but not daily anxieties. The worries are like this: "Shun was a person, and I am a person. Shun was a model for the whole world that could be passed down to future generations, yet I am still nothing more than an ordinary person."[20]

"Daily anxieties" are concerns about things that come and go and over which one has little control—things like professional success and wealth. It is not that one shouldn't care at all about such things, but they should not drive us nor structure how we live our lives.

Elsewhere, Mengzi develops the point this way:

> "Seek and you will get it. Abandon it and you will lose it." In this case, seeking helps in getting, because what is sought is within yourself. "There is a Way to seek it, but getting it depends on fate." In this case, seeking does not help in getting, because what is sought is outside yourself.[21]

We'll discuss the Confucian notion of "fate" quite a bit later; here, our focus is on the idea that we should be motivated by "life-long worries" instead of "daily anxieties." Indeed, on-going, "life-long worries" match up very well with the idea of "commitment" that we have been exploring. Developing a commitment is not easy, but it is much more under your control than is external success. As Mengzi says, in these cases "seeking helps in getting, because what is sought is within yourself."

The notion of life-long worries probably sounds depressing. Sure, Confucians teach us to avoid "daily anxieties," but isn't a life plagued by "worry" still unattractive? In response, let's turn to other sorts of motivations which "pull" us forward and to their connection with the stable sense of joy and ease which accompanies mature commitment. These pulls are in some ways the flip side of the pushes. It's not just that one feels badly about not yet coming close to Shun; one also feels inspired by—that is, pulled toward—him. And it is not just role models like Shun (or Kongzi at age seventy) that draw us on. Classical Confucians like Mengzi write of feeling interconnection with all things and with Heaven; recall, for example, his statement that "All things are complete in oneself. There is no greater joy than to look within and find oneself to be sincere." Neo-Confucians like Zhu Xi take such ideas much further, arguing that is possible to glimpse the manner in which all things can fit harmoniously together, and even to attain a cognitive-emotional state of "unimpeded interconnection" in which the apt ways to respond to any given situation will arise naturally—that is, to become a sage.[22]

Is this Confucian notion of commitment a religious idea? Is it really something like "faith" that is needed to pull one ever onward? Let's recall, after all, the loose sort of Christianity underlying the structure of commitment that Alcoholics Anonymous promotes (as previously stated, step three is "Made a decision to turn our will and our lives over to the care of God as we understood Him"). Does Confucian commitment similarly rest on religious faith?

The answer to this question is going to turn out to depend on what we mean by "religious faith." It's important to understand a few basic things about Confucians and religion. First, like their peers around the world, pre-modern Confucians had a range of beliefs about ghosts, spirits, and other mysterious forces. Second, the focus of Confucianism has always been on our lives here and now. When someone asks Kongzi about serving spirits and about death, he replies, "You are not yet able to serve people; how could you be able to serve ghosts and spirits?" and, "You do not yet understand life; how could you possibly understand death?"[23] Third, there are important ideas within Confucianism that have a religious resonance, most obviously "*tian*," a word that has been translated as "Heaven" and as "cosmos." Early in Chinese history *tian* was the name of a sky god (the basic meaning of the word is "sky") but by the time of Kongzi it had come to have a looser meaning. Modern scholars continue to debate the details, but the consensus view is that references to *tian* signal the acceptance of a cosmos that ultimately has meaning and value, not because of the actions of an agent outside the system (a creator) but because the meaning and value are intrinsically bound up in the on-going generation of the cosmos itself.[24]

This is the context in which "pull" motivations can be based on glimpsing the possibility of broader harmony—broader than just seeing a way that two friends' dispute can be resolved, for all that may be important. This is not based on an unreasoned "leap," like certain versions of "faith," but has a basis in one's own experiences (as well as what one has heard and read about the experiences of others), even though it outruns the experiences and evidence one actually has. Think back to the feeling of "reverence": the awe and joy sparked by feeling one's place among fellow humans as well as the beauties of nature. The Confucian commitment, then, can be seen as an effort to identify oneself as a part of this value-laden cosmos with responsibilities to help to more fully actualize one's own (and the cosmos's own) moral potential. This is, I think, a kind of religiosity—seeing sacredness and value all around you.

Many contemporary studies of moral exemplars have found that religion plays a significant role in the formation of commitment. Some of this research—all conducted on European or American subjects—takes a basically Christian orientation for granted, but one study stands out for adopting a broader stance. The authors of this latter book also talk of religion, but they explain that at the core of the attitudes driving their subjects, they "heard a thrumming concern for a future in which life, 'the most basic, bottom stuff' could flourish—as though they were responding to some call from Life to realize Itself more fully through them."[25] This is precisely the "pull" that Confucians hear and which helps to ground their commitment.

12 | FAKE IT 'TILL YOU MAKE IT

The night after Donald Trump's inauguration, Indian-American comedian Aziz Ansari hosted *Saturday Night Live*. During his opening monologue, Ansari addressed himself to those people he imagined were now saying to themselves, "We don't have to pretend like we're not racists anymore" and proceeding to shout, "Trump won, go back to Africa!" at people of color like Ansari. "No," Ansari responded, "please go back to pretending! . . . I'm sorry we never thanked you for your service. We never realized how much effort you were putting into pretending!"[1] Like his whole monologue, this was funny but also insightful, because pretending really matters—and sometimes it does take a lot of effort.

Pretending is not enough, of course, and sometimes it can be a real problem. Confucians also have lots to say about the problems that hypocrisy can bring. But some forms of pretending—forcing oneself to act correctly, which I will call acting "conscientiously"—are valuable both in the short term and in their longer-term contributions to one's moral growth. Confucians call upon us to strive to be sincere and sagelike, but they recognize the need for quite a lot of pretending along the way.

* * *

What does it mean to "make it"? Why is it so desirable? Remember Kongzi at seventy, who could "follow his heartmind's desires without overstepping the bounds of propriety"? This is having a "mature commitment": one spontaneously does the right thing, flawlessly, without internal struggle. Maturity is obviously something that comes in degrees. What fraction of one's behavior is spontaneous, instead of forced? When you need to force yourself, how hard of a struggle is it to act well? The answers to these questions will change day-to-day, over time, and depend on different life circumstances. Most people act pretty well most of the time, and a lot of that is on the spontaneous end of the spectrum. Yesterday when you brushed your teeth, or hugged your spouse, or did the dishes, did you (or someone else) have to nudge you to do it, or did it simply happen? Less-routine actions can also happen more or less spontaneously; Confucian texts sometimes spell out the degree of moral development one has reached at least partly in terms of how automatically one responds. Why do Confucians put such emphasis on the value of spontaneity?

The most basic problem with non-spontaneous behavior is that it is unreliable. Suppose you cannot avoid spending time with someone whom you find annoying—maybe a coworker, maybe a relative. You know that things will go more smoothly if you keep your frustration to yourself; experience with this person has shown you that you are not the right person to help them overcome the traits that set you off. So long as you really focus, you can pretend to be getting along. But what about an unguarded moment? Furthermore, this kind of sustained pretending can be exhausting. As we have seen, "paying attention" really is draining and can undermine our motivation; at a certain point you can't avoid rolling your eyes and muttering, "Oh, I give up!" Next, even if things do not go this far, to the extent that it is obvious that you are forcing yourself to be nice, that undermines the effect of the nice behavior. Finally, it is also possible that forced pretending may produce less flexible responses than spontaneity would. If you don't really "get it" and are forcing yourself to respond based on a kind of script, you are like a novice actor who does nothing more than what her screenplay indicates. You'll have no way to know what to do if things go "off script." Contrast this with a skilled actor who has learned to really inhabit a role. Both actors are pretending, of course, but the novice's rigid, rule-bound approach leaves a lot to be desired on the stage as in real life.

Natural, spontaneous reactions are the opposite of pretending in each of these respects. Spontaneity is reliable, undemanding, and thus sustainable, genuine, and flexible. It is no surprise, then, that Confucians seek to cultivate "mature commitment" through many of the means discussed in this book. Still, Confucians also tell us to be conscientious (i.e., work to fake it well); as Mengzi says, "Nothing will get one closer to humaneness than to force oneself to act out sympathetic understanding."[2] As this quote implies, conscientiousness is best understood as a learner's virtue: something that we need along the way but hope to eventually get beyond. This is a lot like a student who is good at doing his homework: the point of such dedication is to internalize skills and attitudes such that one no longer needs to care about homework.

Moral learners need conscientiousness because it helps them to have productive interactions with others, as imagined in Ansari's monologue, even if it doesn't do this as well as spontaneous, mature concern for others would. Why does even forced politeness increase the odds of a constructive result? One reason is a sort of double-negative: the absence of rudeness means that conversations are not interrupted. This doesn't guarantee a positive outcome, but it preserves the possibility of learning from one another. It's also true that others' adopting polite or compassionate stances can positively encourage us to respond in kind. This is a special case of a more general phenomenon that Confucians have long recognized and modern social psychologists have been exploring for decades: namely, the details of situations we encounter can significantly influence how we respond. Just to give one example, from Xunzi: by ornamenting a corpse and heaping it with sweet-smelling flowers, our natural instinct to feel disgust is tamped down and we are better able to mourn.[3] In a wide variety of cases, consciously controlling a situation has a positive effect on one's spontaneous reactions, helping them to more reliably attain the feelings and behaviors that we associate with virtue. When you are interacting with someone else, you and your expressions are part of the "situation" they encounter. Controlling yourself shapes the situational context they are in, and thus influences their own reactions.

Does a spontaneous good reaction that only happens because of some detail about a situation count as having "made it"? It's easy to imagine that most people will automatically be respectful to a stranger if the stranger is dressed in business attire but might be less respectful to someone dressed in rags. Obviously, what the other person is wearing is outside our control and, furthermore, shouldn't determine whether we respect them. But for most of us, it will make a difference, just as other aspects of a situation can—like whether we just got paid, are stressed, are in an unfamiliar location, and so on. Wouldn't it be better and more reliable to be able to respond well spontaneously no matter what the context or provocation? Intuitively, the answer to the question must be yes, but we'd also worry about a philosophy that put all its eggs in that basket—that is, if a philosophy told us that only those who can respond perfectly in any situation are good people. After all, such a state of perfection must be rare, if it is even possible. Happily, Confucianism offers very good guidance here. On the one hand, Confucians maintain that the rarified state of sagehood is indeed possible: humans can, in principle, become like Kongzi at age seventy. Nothing I have read from the modern psychological literature shows that sagehood is not possible. On the other hand, while we should always be striving to improve ourselves, edging closer toward the ideal of sagehood, Confucian teachers recognize that neither they nor the rest of us actually are sages. To one degree or another, we are reliant on rituals, music, the encouragement of others, and on our own conscientiousness. We are all learners, at least partly "faking it."

There is a downside to all this faking. For all they recognize the value of conscientiousness, Confucians are also deeply worried about hypocrisy. In the *Analects*, we read that Kongzi considered all of the following shameful: "clever words, an ingratiating countenance, and perfunctory gestures of respect, as well as concealing one's resentment and feigning friendship."[4] In a somewhat later passage, Kongzi wonders: "If someone seems sincere and serious in his conversation, does this mean he is an exemplary person? Or has he merely adopted the appearance of an exemplary person?"[5] Similar themes can be found in other Confucian writings. After all, the hypocrite and the conscientious person resemble one another very closely in both external behavior and much of their inner psychology. The difference seems to lie in two factors: the consistency with which a conscientious person both tries, and succeeds, in getting him or herself to follow duty; and the degree to which the conscientious person is aiming at the higher goal of fuller virtue. A hypocrite is ultimately selfish, interested in appearing good only for ulterior motives. A fascinating subtheme in Confucian treatments of conscientiousness, therefore, is a preference for those who stumble a bit but whose foibles reveal their good intentions, as opposed to someone whose superficially flawless formality risks being devoid of real emotion.[6] In any event, because the temptations of hypocrisy are all too real, "faking it" will always retain a somewhat ambiguous status in Confucian eyes: inevitable and potentially useful for the learners in all of us, but never enough and eternally risky.

* * *

Confucians have a technical term that they use to identify when someone is not faking: "sincerity." One is sincere to the extent that one's inner states (one's desires and feelings) match up with one's outer states (one's expressions and behavior), so it is the opposite of conscientiousness or (worse yet) hypocrisy. Mengzi lauds sincerity when he writes, "There is no greater joy than to look within and find oneself to be sincere."[7] Later Confucians like Zhu Xi pay even more attention to sincerity, connecting it with wholeness, purity, truthfulness, genuineness, unendingness, and spontaneity.[8] Sincerity is such an important topic in Confucianism that we should consider it carefully and critically; to do so, let's look at some challenges to the idea of sincerity that come from a fascinating book called *Ritual and Its Consequences: An Essay on the Limits of Sincerity*. The authors of this book agree with and in fact draw upon the Confucian emphasis on ritual, but they criticize the idea of sincerity as unrealistic and even bad for us. For them, living a good life involves accepting that there is no "making it": we just need to keep on faking. By looking into the ways that Confucians can respond to such concerns, we gain a deeper sense of what a Confucian life really entails.

For the authors of *Ritual and Its Consequences*, to be sincere means "to resolve all ambiguity [and] forge a pure and unsullied consciousness."[9] The problem is that our world is "fractured" or "broken"; they say that ritual, play, and music all aim at creating counter-factual, pretend wholeness "in overt tension with the world of lived experience."[10] The aim of ritual or music, therefore, is "not to achieve perfection but to recall it while living in an unperfectible world."[11] Against this background, they frame sincerity as committed to a kind of fundamentalism, according to which conceptions of enlightenment or perfection that should perhaps be understood as transcending the material world are re-interpreted as taking place within human history and society. In this way, the quest for sincerity can demand a "unidirectional sense of self-purpose" and the (inevitable) result of failing to achieve such a purpose is self-loathing.[12]

There is obviously much worth discussing in this rich book, but for our purposes the key is to see how some of the authors' assumptions differ from those of the Confucians we have encountered. Historical Confucians believed that things were better back when the ancient sage-kings ruled than during the present day (whether the "present day" was the Warring States of Mengzi or the Song Dynasty of Zhu Xi), but things are worse today not because the world has been "broken." There is no Fall, no original sin; neither is there a single Creation of a world that can then be broken. Confucians instead imagine a continual process of the generation of life. Changes, cycles, patterns, and polarities are the deep metaphors of Confucian thinking about the cosmos. There is no room here for the rigid idea of a static, perfect whole which then fractures.

Sincerity and perfection thus mean different things in this Confucian cosmos than they do in the world of *Ritual and Its Consequences*. Perfect sincerity and pure sagehood are extraordinarily rare and perhaps even temporary achievements, but nothing makes them impossible. More importantly, sincerity is something that comes in degrees and which we can get better at; much of this book is about the process of working to cultivate the ability to sincerely respond to the way the world really is. And that world is complex and changing. The last thing that Confucians are interested in is a "unidirectional sense of self-purpose," unless that purpose is the encompassing one of striving for sagehood.

Even though Confucian exemplary people have sincere and deep commitments to morality, they differ in crucial ways from radicals committed to a cause who see the world through a single set of ideological categories.[13] The radical's consistency may seem impressive, but genuine attention to the details of particular people and events demands a more nuanced response. Consistency can come at the cost of extirpating concern for anything but the cause; by denying the crucial values that come from our connections to one another, radicals deny their full humanity. It is true that to the extent we "make it" (no longer needing to "fake it"), we have undergone a kind of transformation, but our more exemplary selves continue to honor all the values and relationships on which our human place in the cosmos depends. Doing this means expanding rather than denying the self.

13 | EXPANDING THE SELF

I have a problem with gated communities. (You might have noticed this already.) Some of my relatives have lived for years in a gated community which we've visited periodically. Not only is their residential area gated; the main park in their town is also gated, and only local residents are issued keys to get in.[1] We could debate whether or not, as Robert Frost wrote, "good fences make good neighbors."[2] But gates go beyond setting out boundaries; they enforce separation and disconnection. As we saw, disconnection cultivates what Iris Murdoch calls "fantasy": "the tissue of self-aggrandizing and consoling wishes and dreams which prevents one from seeing what is there outside one." In Confucian terms, disconnection breeds "selfishness," the problem at the core of most vice and one that, I'd argue, gated communities make worse by tightening one's circle of concern and closing out others.

The extreme opposite of selfishness is selflessness, an attitude that many moralists have lauded. Murdoch writes approvingly of the "humble man" who, "because he sees himself as nothing, can see others as they really are."[3] Consider also the case of Zell

Kravinsky, who has given away virtually all of the millions he made in real estate and donated a kidney to a stranger, but still feels deeply pained by his inability (and his society's unwillingness) to do more. In an interview he said, "What I aspire to is ethical ecstasy. *Ex Stasis*: standing out of myself, where I'd lose my punishing ego. It's tremendously burdensome to me."[4] There is much to admire about Kravinsky, undoubtedly, but to live out Confucian ideals we should neither disconnect from others nor from ourselves, but rather build on the connectedness we sense. No Confucian could say, as Kravinsky does, "I don't know that two children should die so that one of my kids lives."[5] Nonetheless, we'll see that the Confucian teaching that we "form one body with all things" can have profound effects on how we live our lives and order our societies, even leading to a kind of ecological consciousness, albeit one in which our human lives still feature prominently.

* * *

Let's start with Confucian opposition to self*less*ness. Mengzi once had a conversation with a king who admitted to weaknesses like fondness for wealth and sex. Rather than tell the king that he had to deny himself if he was to become a true leader, Mengzi explains that the king can enjoy his pleasures so long as his people can enjoy theirs as well. (Admittedly, this will mean the king restraining himself somewhat: if he pays all his attention to amassing wealth or concubines, he neglects his responsibilities to his people who then end up destitute and alone.) Mengzi puts the point more abstractly in one of the key passages from *Mengzi*. I often tell my students that if you can understand this passage, you've got Mengzi figured out. Here it is:

> The mouth in relation to flavors, the eyes in relation to sights, the ears in relation to notes, the nose in relation to odors, the four limbs in relation to comfort: these are matters of nature but they are also fated. Nonetheless, an exemplary person does not refer to them as "nature." Humaneness between father and son, righteousness between ruler and minister, propriety between guest and host, wisdom in relation to the worthy . . . : these are fated, but they also involved nature. Nonetheless, an exemplary person does not refer to them as "fated."[6]

Mengzi distinguishes between two sets of inclinations: physical ones (like our desire for tasty flavors) and moral ones (like the tendency of parents and children to interact with humane care). The moral inclinations are what Mengzi elsewhere calls our "sprouts." He also distinguishes in this passage between a tendency's being our "nature" and being "fated." For Mengzi, "fate" refers to things outside our control. Our mouths are drawn toward sweetness more or less from birth; we do not have to do anything to make this so. This is "fate." If you lose your job because the company goes bankrupt and everyone is laid off, this is also fate since it is outside your control. "Nature," on the other hand, refers here to the best self that a thing has the built-in (i.e., natural) potential to become. In this sense, it is an acorn's "nature" to be an oak tree—and a human's nature to be an "exemplary person."

How does all this relate to selflessness and so on? According to the passage, exemplary people refer only to our moral tendencies as "nature," but Mengzi acknowledges that our physical tendencies are also part of our "nature." This is obviously very compressed; here's what's going on. Both moral and physical tendencies arise in us on their own (think of the reaction to seeing a baby about to fall into a well) and so are "fated," but the physical ones are much more robust than the moral ones. If we do nothing to nurture our moral reactions, they'll remain weak and will rarely move us to action. This is why we need to "cultivate" our sprouts. Physical reactions, on the other hand, don't need our help. Sure, you can cultivate a taste for something new or learn to appreciate subtle distinctions of flavor, but even without this, you'll enjoy food. So exemplary people focus their efforts on the moral reactions, and Mengzi signals this by saying they don't actively think of the physical ones as "nature." Still—and this is crucial for our purposes—physical satisfactions are nonetheless part of our nature, part of our best lives. Living a good Confucian life involves physical pleasures as well as moral ones: we can and should enjoy good food and drink, so long as such pleasures don't distract us, at least for too long, from the world outside our dining room. In short, Confucians do not deny the (physical) self, so they do not advocate selflessness. Their emphasis is not on the physical self, but it is important that it comes along for the ride.

As for self*ish*ness, pretty much everyone acts selfishly now and again, and we all know people who do so often. They seem not to care about others' concerns, or perhaps their own viewpoint and desires so dominate what they can see that others' issues are tiny and irrelevant in comparison. Selfishness is distinguishing oneself from others in inappropriate ways by over-weighting one's own concerns or under-weighting those of others, often by excluding them or separating oneself from them. Wang Yangming explains that while feelings like "pleasure, anger, joy, and sorrow in themselves are naturally in equilibrium and harmony, as soon as one attaches a bit of one's own idea to them, they will be excessive or deficient, which is to say that they will be selfish."[7] In Wang's view, selfishness interrupts the natural unity of stimulus and response. Instead of reacting to the real situation in front of one, one "attaches a bit of one's own idea," which is to say one twists the situation in some way. One example is when one comes up with excuses not to do something: one ignores the real situation because it is easier or more convenient at the moment to do so. One can often talk oneself into not seeing the world as it really is. Even more relevantly—because selfishness often operates automatically—aspects of one's background may intercede unconsciously. We are probably all familiar by now with the problem of unconscious bias. When you unwittingly find yourself preferring a job candidate who looks like you or sounds like you, despite your avowed intention to be neutral, you are being selfish. Tests of unconscious bias reveal how ubiquitous this is, but as we learn more, we also come to see ways in which this form of selfishness can be deconstructed.[8]

Wang's point is that there are no desires or feelings that are intrinsically selfish. (This is just like Mengzi saying that all desires are part of our "nature.") Selfishness therefore depends on context. Ignoring others when they are relevant results in selfish actions. We can connect this to modern psychological research via the idea of "moral disengagement." Albert Bandura has explored the ways in which "[t]he self-regulatory mechanisms governing moral conduct do not come into play unless they are activated, and there are many psychosocial maneuvers by which moral self-sanctions are selectively disengaged from inhumane conduct."[9] Imagine yourself walking along a downtown street and noticing a panhandler ahead of you. What happens next? Do you busy yourself with your cell phone, develop a sudden interest in something on the other side of the street, or simply stare firmly ahead as you pass him by? Most of us will find some way to avoid eye contact, avoid engagement, maybe backing this up with the thought that he's probably lying and doesn't really need our help. When I say that selfishness (or disengagement) explains how we can do immoral or inhumane things, I don't just mean giant injustices; selfishness and its attendant immoralities are everyday affairs.

* * *

So, what should we do instead? Where selfishness cuts others off from the self and selflessness cuts oneself out of consideration, the Confucian approach throughout the tradition has been to expand the self. I previously noted that Mengzi asks us to reflect on how we have responded to events in our day, and then seek to "extend" those reactions about which we feel good to other circumstances in which we are less proud of how we responded. While it's easy to feel compassion for a baby, you may find it harder to treat a panhandler like a person in need. Confucian writings about extension aim to help us see and feel the similarities in these situations, though, and thus ultimately to help us treat them similarly. Mengzi writes: "Treat your elders as elders, and extend it to the elders of others; treat your young ones as young ones, and extend it to the young ones of others."[10]

A critical question is whether we should understand this kind of extension as expanding the self, or just expanding of the sphere of others—that is, non-self—for whom one cares. In fact, we've already seen that Mengzi defines "sincerity" in terms of inclusive self: "All things are complete in oneself. There is no greater joy than to look within and find oneself to be sincere."[11] Neo-Confucians expand on this theme with a powerful metaphor first introduced by one of Zhu Xi's predecessors named Cheng Hao (1032–1085 CE). He writes:

> Medical books describe paralysis in the hands or feet as being "numb or unfeeling." This is a perfect way to describe the condition. People with feeling (i.e., humane people) regard heaven, earth, and the myriad things as one body; there is nothing that is not part of themselves. Since they regard all things as themselves, is there anywhere their concern will fail to reach? If things are not parts of oneself, naturally they will have no influence upon one. This is like hands and feet being unfeeling; the vital stuff no longer circulates through and connects them, and so they no longer are parts of the self.[12]

According to Cheng Hao, that is, one "feels" for others because they are connected to one—are part of one's self. Having "feeling" for another is both literal (experiencing something) and ethical (being concerned for them).

In many cultures it's natural to think that one's "self" is basically the same as one's body. We're "connected" to our hands and feet, but not connected in the same way to a different person. Still, often it does seem that we "feel" pain when another person is in distress. Psychologists have studied such reactions and have tended to label them as instances of "empathy": that is, "having the feelings of another (involuntarily) aroused in ourselves."[13] Importantly, though, other researchers have shown that concern for another is related to the degree to which one sees similarities between the other and oneself, which they refer to as the degree of "oneness."[14] What this means is that someone whom we think of as being very empathic is simultaneously someone who perceives a broader connection—or oneness—with others than does the average person. The fact that oneness underlies concern for others makes evolutionary sense: to the extent that my group flourishes, so do I (and my genes). This also means, however, that insofar as I do not see someone as one with me, I am less likely to respond to their plight with care.

The reason that expanding one's sense of self is important, then, is that this is the key to expanding the sphere of others for whom one cares. Some philosophers and psychologists in the West have recognized this.[15] As I have been saying, Confucians have long understood this, and further understood that our goal should not be a complete merging of self with the cosmos. Some distinctions remain important to our lives. So, when Wang Yangming tells us to "form one body with all things," he adds that there are still degrees of importance:

> If we use the hands and the feet to protect the head, does that mean that we go too far in treating them as less important? This simply accords with their Pattern. We love both plants and animals, yet we can bear nurturing animals with plants.

We love both animals and humans, and yet we can bear butchering animals to feed our parents, provide for sacrifices, and entertain guests. We love both parents and strangers. But suppose here are a small basket of rice and a bowl of soup. With them one will survive and without them one will die; there is not enough to save both parent and stranger. We can bear preferring to save the parent instead of the stranger.[16]

Setting aside for now Wang's reference to "Pattern," we see that the way Wang envisions "one body" includes caring for all things, but also accepting that not everything is equally important. We do care for hands, plants, animals, and strangers: to the extent that they are used to nourish or protect other aspects of our "self," we feel badly but can "bear" this pain. It's obviously better if our hands don't have to suffer because we never trip and fall, and if no one starves because there is enough food for all. The main thing the passage is telling us, though, is that the Confucian vision of oneness admits of gradations.

Certain types of relationships are central to our selfhood—to who we are—and other types are more peripheral, even if they also matter. Mengzi put this in terms of five canonical relationships: between parent and child, between ruler and subject, between elder and younger sibling, between husband and wife, and between friend and friend.[17] Four of these five relationships were traditionally marked by a status differentiation or "hierarchy"; you will read more about these ideas, and problems with them, in Chapters 18 and 19. The key for now is to understand that Confucians understand that our intimate, familial relationships are—and should be—the foundation of who we are. We sometimes selfishly over-emphasize distinctive aspects of our familial, ethnic, national, or gender identity, but to insist on a selfless equivalence among all people would be to reject the very bedrock of our humanity.

Still, we might well wonder: Wouldn't it be better not to "butcher" part of our "selves"? To sharpen this question, let's look at the most famous Confucian statement about our place in the cosmos, the opening of Zhang Zai (1020–1077 C.E.)'s *Western Inscription*:

> Heaven is my father and earth is my mother, and even such a small creature as I finds an intimate place in their midst. Therefore that which fills the universe I regard as my body and that which directs the universe I regard as my nature. All people are my brothers and sisters, and all things are my companions.[18]

Fully unpacking these few lines would take a whole book in itself, but it should be clear that Zhang Zai does not think of aspects of the cosmos outside his physical form as fundamentally separate from him, for him to use however he likes. Instead, he is part of a larger, differentiated whole. There is still hierarchy here: heaven and earth have a higher status than he does, because they are akin to his parents; other people are like siblings; and the rest of the cosmos are "companions." Zhang uses the analogy of human roles to understand the cosmos, so we can say that his vision relies essentially on his human standpoint and ways of valuing. Because humans have a distinctive but not uniquely high value in this scheme, the eminent modern Confucian scholar Tu Wei-ming suggests that we call it "anthropocosmic" rather than the more typical "anthropocentric."[19]

We're left with something of a puzzle. On the one hand, the Confucian vision of oneness can be extremely expansive, providing us a straight-forward way to think about the value of non-human animals and even of non-sentient aspects of our environment: they are all, ultimately, parts of ourselves, even if they are less central than other parts. This has the potential to ground a deep ecological consciousness, and some individual Confucians did write movingly of their own connection with their environment. On the other hand, historically Confucianism never became an environmentalist movement—for example, worrying about the effects of deforestation or urbanization. And Confucians from Kongzi and Mengzi down to Wang Yangming have taken it for granted that it is appropriate to eat meat. The historical explanations for these facts are pretty clear. Individual connectedness to nature did not translate into systematic study of changing ecosystems, I think, because the focus of Confucian theorizing has always been more on individual development than on systems or institutions. As for meat-eating, note that Wang Yangming explained it as needed to "feed our parents, provide for sacrifices, and entertain guests." In other words, meat eating served important ritual purposes, and the value of these rituals was enough that one could "bear" the grief of killing animals.

Should Confucians of today view things in the same way? Taking oneness seriously means adopting an anthropocosmic stance and seeing all things as having value. This is not the same as saying that all life is "sacred" nor that all life has "equal" value, as some other environmentalist stances might. Meat-eating probably does not have the same ritual function for you as it did for traditional Chinese; does it have some other significance for you? If we are to "bear" certain things, we should at least be aware of what the butchering of animals entails. Friends of mine run a small farm and their daughter has long held to the maxim that she will not eat meat from animals she did not raise herself: she knows they lived good lives and did not suffer when killed. I do not think there is a one-size-fits-all Confucian answer for meat-eating, but as we extend our selves we must each grapple with questions like this. As for broader issues of environmentalism, armed with tools from the environmental sciences, Confucians must of course be environmentalists, seeking a harmony in which humans can live good lives in the context of a flourishing natural world.

14 | DEALING WITH CONFLICT

The level of corruption in China today is around the world's average.[1] Even if it is not as bad as in Somalia or Venezuela, corruption is a concern for many in China. According to some Chinese pundits, Confucianism is to blame. They worry about the degree to which Confucianism teaches nepotism. One passage from the *Analects* is regularly cited as evidence for this problem:

The Duke of She said to Kongzi, "Among my people there is one we call Upright Gong. When his father stole a sheep, he reported him to the authorities."

Kongzi replied, "Among my people, those whom we consider upright are different from this: fathers cover up for their sons, and sons cover up for their fathers. Uprightness is to be found in this."[2]

Scholars debate about exactly what Kongzi's reply means. Is the idea to cover up for familial crime in all cases, and never do anything about it? Or does it depend on how serious a crime it is (and was sheep-stealing serious, or not, in Kongzi's day?)? These are interesting questions, but they largely miss the point of the key philosophical question raised by the passage: Namely, how should we deal with moral conflicts? The truth is that the story of Upright Gong by itself is too brief to be of that much help.

Luckily, other Confucian texts explore the theme of conflicts between different values more thoroughly. The most revealing case comes from *Mengzi* and concerns the sage-king Shun and his step-brother Xiang. Xiang, as you will see, is not a good guy:

A student said, "Xiang devoted himself every day to plotting against Shun's life. Why did Shun only banish him when he became Emperor?"

Mengzi replied, "He enfeoffed him. Some called this banishment."

"Shun banished various villains; Xiang was the most wicked of them all, yet he was enfeoffed in You Bi. What wrong had the people of You Bi done? Is that the way a humane man behaves? Others he punishes, but when it comes to his own brother he enfeoffs him instead."

Mengzi replied, "A humane man never harbors anger or nurses a grudge against a brother. All he does is to love him. Because he loves him, he wishes him to enjoy rank; because he loves him, he wishes him to enjoy wealth. To enfeoff Xiang in You Bi was to let him enjoy wealth and rank. If as Emperor he were to allow his brother to be a nobody, could that be described as loving him?"

"May I ask what you meant by saying that some called this
   banishment?"
"Xiang was not allowed to take any action in his fief. The Emperor
   appointed officials to administer the fief and to collect tributes
   and taxes. For this reason it was described as banishment.
   Xiang was certainly not permitted to ill-use the people."[3]

It seems that Xiang was both honored and punished, depending
on how one looked at it. Faced with the question of whether his
villainous brother should be banished or enfeoffed, Shun found
a way to do both. The ideal Confucian way to deal with conflict,
in short, is to harmonize all the relevant dimensions of value.

* * *

It is natural that Confucians respond to potential conflicts by
looking for harmony because harmony is one of their most deep-
seated values. Before focusing specifically on conflicts, therefore,
let's take a few moments to unpack what Confucians mean by
"harmony." The basic idea is that you have harmony when you
have a combination of complementary differences. Life itself, not
to mention beauty and meaning, depends on diverse elements fitting together. As one early text says, "There is no music with one
note, no culture with one object, no satisfactory results with one
flavor."[4] Musical and culinary analogies are common; one of the
most famous compares harmony to a soup:

Harmony is like a broth, wherein water, fire, vinegar, minced
meat, salt, and plum sauce are used to boil fish meat. Cooking

it over firewood, the chef harmonizes it, proportioning it with flavor: adding to what falls short and taking away from what is in excess. Exemplary people partake of it and thereby set their heartminds in balance.[5]

Many texts go on to say that uniformity is as unacceptable in politics as it is in music or cooking. Just as we would not eat a soup of water added to water nor listen to music in which all the instruments struck the same notes, so too is a minister who simply agrees with the ruler—no matter what the ruler says—a failure as a minister.[6] "Yes men" make bad ministers because they fail to play their crucial role of correcting leaders who are tempted to rule in a selfish way. This same theme is expressed more succinctly in the famous *Analects* saying, "The exemplary person is harmonious but not uniform. The petty person is uniform but not harmonious."[7]

Notice that in all these examples, harmony is not just a simple balancing of two things. Many ingredients and activities (the right degree of flame for the right amount of time; the proper stirring) go into making an ideal soup. Achieving harmony is more a matter of skilled judgment than objective calculation. This is all the more true when part of the judgment is deciding which factors are relevant in the first place. Put yourself in Shun's place: you have become emperor and are immediately faced with the question of how to deal with the brother who has treated you so badly. Part of the reason that Shun is known as a sage is his ability to respond to this challenge with such nuance. He loves his brother, he cares for the people in all his realm (including those in You Bi), and he wants to act righteously (and encourage his people to do the same). Furthermore, part of loving his brother is harboring the on-going hope that Xiang matures as a more moral person. Shun's response to these seemingly conflicting demands is exemplary because he both notices all the different dimensions and is able to arrive at the banishment-and-also-enfeoffment solution that does justice to all of them. This is what I mean by harmonizing all the relevant dimensions of value.

I know what you're thinking. You're probably willing to acknowledge that Shun's response was clever and also that his ability to continue to love his brother is impressive; many of us would have sought revenge had we been in Shun's shoes. But your main reaction is that sometimes conflicts cannot be resolved in such neat ways. What about the sheep-stealing father, after all? Doesn't his child have to either turn him in or not?

The Confucian tradition offers us a two-part answer to this question. The first part is to emphasize that thinking outside of the box, seeing dimensions of the problem that others have missed and then using them to arrive at harmony, is part of what it is to be a sage. We all are somewhere on the road toward sagehood (say Confucians) and so in different circumstances will do better or worse at finding a sagely solution. One key item in the sagely toolkit is the fact that harmony is not a one-off balance, but rather an on-going relationship leading to (moral) growth. So, actually, we should not think of harmony as the ways that flavors in a soup or musical notes relate to one another at a single moment, but broaden our frame to include all the dishes in a meal or notes in an entire composition. Applied to a case like sheep-stealing, this means that one needs to take into account a broader context—has your father lost his job and is concerned about his children being able to eat?—as well as whether working with him to reform his ways and perhaps repay the neighbor seems feasible. As we saw in Chapter 3, there are various ways in which one can try to respond constructively to a problematic parent. All of this goes into a judgment about which steps contribute to a "harmonious" response to a given situation.

The second part to an answer is recognizing that even harmonious responses to conflicts often should include emotional recognition that something unfortunate has occurred. Feelings like grief are often appropriate. Confucians are very explicit that negative emotions can be a necessary, constructive part of harmony, and even part of a peculiar form of "joy." There will be more to say about this as it relates to death, but here we can note Wang Yangming's statement, "There is harmony in sorrow. This refers to its taking rise from complete sincerity and being without any affectation. The infant cries all day without hurting his throat. This is the extreme of harmony."[8] Wang makes the same point in a slightly different way when asked whether "joy" is present when one's parent has died and one is crying bitterly. Wang says: "There is real joy only if the son has cried bitterly. If not, there won't be any joy. Joy means that in spite of crying, one's heartmind is at peace."[9] In other words, sorrow that is completely sincere, that manifests complete integrity with one's situation, can be extreme and still harmonious—and can even be a form of joy.

Thinking back to the sheep-stealing incident, we can now see that Kongzi's brief statement about "uprightness" left a lot out. A harmonious response to conflicting values needs to honor all the relevant values, which sometimes means that it will be accompanied by negative emotions. For one more instance of how this can be done, let me adapt an example that the contemporary philosopher Karen Stohr uses to argue against what she calls the "harmony thesis." Stohr thinks that believers in harmony hold that good people "should find virtuous action easy and pleasant."[10] However, she asks us to imagine the case of a small business owner:

> She has a number of employees, all of whom have worked for her for years and all of whom are capable and dependable. Since the company is small, she has gotten to know her employees relatively well and she has developed genuine affection and concern for them. Due to a recent downturn in the economy, demand for the company's products has declined and the company is in financial trouble. After agonizing over the books, the owner of the company has decided that there is no alternative but to lay off several of her employees. She has already taken every other cost-cutting step possible and this is the last remaining option. If she does not perform any layoffs, the company will certainly go under and all her employees will lose their jobs.[11]

Stohr then goes on to describe how the owner will naturally be fair in choosing whom to fire, will break the news in the softest way she can, and so on. We are further to imagine that the owner's sympathy for employees leaves her "anguished by the knowledge that she will be causing them pain and distress."[12] Being sympathetic, that is, makes it harder for her to perform the correct action. Contrary to advocates of her so-called harmony thesis, Stohr says that in a case like this, "it seems to be a requirement of virtue that she finds it hard."[13]

This owner sounds well on the way to being a sage. Confucians should agree with almost every aspect of Stohr's analysis, except for two things. First, we need to clarify what it means to say that the owner "finds it hard" to act virtuously. It hurts to do what she must, and she feels badly for her former employees. No doubt she will strive to re-hire them or give them references and other support, but this doesn't lessen the sadness she feels. Still, she does not have to struggle against herself to do what must be done; she is not wracked with doubt or regrets. Her rightful sorrow motivates her to move forward. Therefore—and this is the second way Confucians will qualify Stohr's conclusion— the owner is still in a state of harmony. Her sorrow is no affectation; in Wang Yangming's words, it "takes rise from complete sincerity."

* * *

But how can she do it? What enables the owner to move forward rather than being crippled by what has happened? Is she really, deep down, somewhat callous if she doesn't find her life marred? I think that Confucian teachings are very helpful here, and the key is understanding and giving the proper (limited!) role to what they call "fate." Here is the early Neo-Confucian Cheng Yi (1033–1107 CE):

> At the time of difficulty, if an exemplary person has done their best but cannot avoid it, that is fate. One should investigate to the utmost their fate in order to fulfill their commitment. Understanding the necessity of fate, one's heartmind will not be disturbed by poverty, obstacles, or calamity. One will merely enact their virtue of righteousness. If one does

not understand fate, they will be afraid when they encounter danger and difficulty and stumble when they suffer poverty, and what they hold on to will be lost. How can such a one fulfill their commitment to do good?[14]

In other words, in addition to conflicts between different values, another kind of conflict lies between things that happen outside of one's control and the way we wish things were. Stohr's business owner really didn't want to economy to tank, forcing her to lay off workers, but it did. As Cheng Yi explains, when you have done your best and difficulty is still unavoidable, that is fate.

The Chinese understanding of fate is quite different from that of the ancient Greeks and Romans. In the ancient Western world, the Fates were goddesses who determined the basic facts of each person's life—how long they'd live, how much joy or suffering they'd experience. These facts about individual lives were predetermined. The Chinese category of *ming* bears enough similarity to this Greek idea that we can still translate it as "fate," but it does not refer to the predetermination of one's life. Instead, *ming* labels all those things that are outside one's control. Born a human, you have various emotional and physical capabilities: this is fate. You lack wings and cannot fly: fate. You're tall or short, fair or dark: fate. And the many things that happen in the world outside your control—droughts or hurricanes, baby booms or economic busts—these are all fate as well. They structure one's options but do not determine all outcomes; after all, as Mengzi says, "Someone who understands fate does not stand beneath a crumbling wall."[15]

Returning to Cheng Yi's statement, we can see that it is accepting of fate without being fatalist. "One should investigate to the utmost their fate in order to fulfill their commitment": in other words, Stohr's business owner should leave no stone unturned as she seeks the best way to respond to her company's plight. If she chooses to lay off workers because of lazily neglecting to find a better way, this is a deep failure on her part (it is, of course, a kind of selfishness). Her "commitment" to being the best person she can be very much includes her relationships with and responsibilities to her employees, so fulfilling that commitment involves doing her best for them, under the circumstances. If the circumstances (that is, fate) give her no other option, with a heavy heart she must lay off some workers. What she cannot do, says Cheng Yi, is become "afraid" or "stumble" in the face of this difficulty. If the layoffs leave her so bereft that she cannot move forward, perhaps obsessively wondering whether she was right to start the business in the first place, then the commitment that she was trying to "hold on to" risks being lost.

There are plenty of ways in which we non-sages can fall short of the ideal Confucian harmonious response to difficulties and conflicts. Maybe we actually were a bit selfish and didn't quite do our best. Maybe we lack the strength and clarity required to distinguish between fate and our own responsibilities. Confucian thinkers address these situations as well; a contemporary scholar has explored some of them in a book called *The Vulnerability of Integrity*.[16] In addition, sometimes it may be ambiguous whether the situation we face is the result of our actions or outside of control. Historically, Confucians debated about what natural portents (like eclipses) or disasters said about the reigning emperor. Some saw such occurrences as indicating a lack of harmony in the cosmos, which they felt was the responsibility of the emperor to maintain. Others like Xunzi explicitly argued that while events like droughts are inevitable, famines are not. Famines come from not preparing properly, not responding to the predictable cycles of nature.[17] Updating this to the present day, we now know that even some of the "natural" events we are facing are the results of human-induced climate change, and thus ultimately are the responsibility of generations of political leaders and other human choices.

Even if it can be difficult to respond to conflicts and other challenges like a sage would, there is still enormous value in holding the sagely response as an ideal and working toward realizing it to the extent that we can. The Confucians are not wrong: there are things that are outside of our control, things that we should grieve about without blaming ourselves. And with some imagination, even non-sages can usually find a way to recognize and honor the different values present in a conflict.

15 | ENLIGHTENMENT AND SAGEHOOD

It might be a bad thing to think you're a sage. Liang Shuming (1893–1988 CE), one of 20th-century China's leading Confucian intellectuals, had a reputation for considering himself "a sage with a capital S." According to his biographer, he was forever trying to act in as moral a way as possible, making his life an on-going battle against the ever-present danger of moral failure. As a result, Liang seldom laughed or even smiled.[1] This description of Liang makes him sound a lot like what philosopher Susan Wolf calls a "moral saint." She is very critical of rigid moral sainthood, writing that "moral saintliness does not constitute a model of personal well-being toward which it would be particularly rational or good or desirable for a human being to strive."[2] Instead, Wolf argues, one can be "perfectly wonderful without being perfectly moral."[3]

Confucians are committed to the idea that sagehood is actually a deeply desirable goal, even though few if any people will reach the state of being a full-on sage. It's vital to understand the difference between striving to be sage-like right now and striving each day to get closer to the ideal. Both Liang's version of sagehood and Wolf's idea of moral saint suffer from their narrow focus on a particular idea of morality. Confucian sagehood, in contrast, is a personality ideal that pays inclusive attention to all sorts of values. The road toward sagehood may include enlightenment experiences, but sagehood itself is not a radically different state from non-sagehood.

* * *

To better understand what sagehood means to Confucians, we should start in what may seem like an unlikely place: ancient Greece. Ideas of sagehood in Greece are often bound up with a conception of divinity, which is a realm of perfection separate from humanity. Only gods are truly wise, though humans can and should aspire after wisdom (*sophia*); those who do so are lovers of *sophia*, or "philosophers." Because these individuals love and aspire to something that is fundamentally different from our limited human knowledge, though, Greek theorists generally recognize that its pursuit requires a break with everyday life. For many Greek thinkers, the best human life is the life of contemplation (*theoria*),[4] even though it seems impossible to actually live a human life as a sage (or *sophos*). The exact kind of impossibility differs depending on the specific Greek thinker: Plato believes that as long as one has a physical body, one cannot attain *sophia*, whereas Aristotle does seem to think it is possible to attain *sophia*, but the life in question will be bizarre and "useless" from a human perspective.[5] Much of Aristotle's writing on ethics, therefore, focuses on the *phronimos*, the "practically wise" person who lives a virtuous and well-rounded life. Scholars of Aristotle debate about how the ideals of sagehood and practical wisdom are supposed to relate to one another; I find most plausible Jiyuan Yu's conclusion: in Aristotle's vision, "the fulfillment of the practical self does not lead to the fulfillment of the theoretical self, and vice-versa. These are two models of human flourishing that cannot be fulfilled within a single career."[6]

Coming along several centuries later but drawing on classical Greek as well as Roman traditions, Christian saints also occupy a framework that makes perfection impossible for humans. Perfection is the realm of God and the angels. This impossibility translates into extraordinary demands that are placed on the saint to get as close as possible to an unattainable ideal. Andrew Flescher has written insightfully about saints in both religious and secular contexts, and concludes that

> theirs is an excessive morality that begins from an already expanded sense of duty and extends to their total submission to the face of the Other. Saints are disposed to go beyond any robust sense of moral requirement, indeed to the very limit of what they can manage.[7]

Flescher discusses modern exemplars like Martin Luther King, Jr., and Dorothy Day, who seem to have understood themselves in very much this way, noting that the excessiveness to which they were prone "made them incurably anxious, barring them from ever considering their work completed, and in turn, rendering them ineligible for living comfortably in any social environment not dominated by the recurring human crises that so fiercely occupied their attention."[8] These real-life examples help to flesh out Susan

Wolf's argument that while the "maximal devotion" of such saints to morality is admirable, it is much less tempting to say that we should or even could model our own lives on their examples.[9] In other words, we can honor and respect the accomplishments of moral saints like King, but there are real questions about whether we should strive to model ourselves on their lives.

The maximal devotion of saints may remind you of the "life-long worries" that Mengzi thinks are important—such as worrying that one falls short of Shun's inspiring example—but there is a critical difference. The understanding of "morality" on which such "moral saints" are based is much narrower than the broad spectrum of values that Confucians recognize as relevant to good, virtuous lives. Most importantly, a rich and caring family life is central to Confucian flourishing; contrast this to "saints" who ignore or even reject close ties in order to devote themselves to helping others. (Think of Zell Kravinsky who questioned giving his child preference over a stranger.) There are always ways in which Confucians can be better than we are currently, but the options for our lives are much richer and more balanced than for saints. In response to the difficulty of living as a saint, in fact, many strands of Western moral thinking explicitly deny that we have any responsibility to be like the saints. According to these ways of thinking, morality places on us certain, limited moral duties. These duties are mainly or even exclusively related to our treatment of others: things like not harming others and not lying. One can go beyond these duties (as saints do), but this is optional; the technical term for going beyond one's duties is "supererogation."

* * *

The Confucian approach to sages and to the demands of morality (or ethics; I use the two interchangeably) is quite different. It is based in a broader conception of morality, as just noted; and it revolves around the idea of continuity, in several senses:

- There is a continuum of moral growth from "petty person" to "committed learner" to "exemplary person" to "sage." We each have the possibility of gradually improving.
- Each level of moral improvement is accessible to us, at least in principle. This is because the lives lived by "committed learners," "exemplary people," and even "sages" are continuous with—that is, recognizably similar to—our own.
- Ethical demands on each of us are continuous. There is no point where we can stop, resting on our laurels. We can always be better: Confucians do not recognize the idea of supererogation. They do accept, though, that we neither can nor should instantly become full sages, and so we need not criticize ourselves for that failure.

This is a lot to grasp, especially if you are a total newcomer to Confucianism, so let's break it all down, piece-by-piece.

There is no systematic agreement over the whole range of Confucian texts on how exactly to label the stages of moral growth, but the general idea here is common property. Some early texts primarily use "exemplary person" as their target and rarely speak of the "sage," but this is just a matter of historical development of what the term "sage" means.[10] Xunzi gives us a particularly insightful discussion of stages, though he is also not completely consistent in his terms. Synthesizing a few different passages from *Xunzi*, we can find the following levels:

- The "common mass of humanity" or the "petty people." Even though they may find it useful to appear good and public-spirited, they often have "crooked and selfish" motives.
- "Committed scholars." They are committed to "repressing the merely private and thus are able to be public-spirited"; they strive to follow "models" of good behavior but often act "too rigidly" in following these models.
- "Exemplary people." These individuals are able to "embody the model"; their "conduct is generally appropriate, but they are not yet fully at ease."
- Sages, finally, are "at ease with what is public-spirited."[11]

These ideas resonate well with the account of moral growth presented thus far, especially as seen in the "fake it 'till you make it" framework: we start by committing ourselves to follow external standards, and gradually our virtuous dispositions develop so that we can more closely approximate the ease with which Confucius acted at age seventy.

The second sense in which we are continuous with sages is that each of the levels of improvement is accessible, at least in principle, to any one of us. What I mean by "in principle" here is that exemplary people and sages are not fundamentally different from you and me. Mengzi makes this explicit: "We and the sages are of the same kind. . . . The sages first discovered what our heartminds prefer in common."[12] That is, the full range of human concerns and values that are relevant in our current lives continue to be relevant as we improve. Family life, beauty, physical pleasure, and so on are all still values for sages as well, even if sages do not put particular emphasis on some of them. Sages are not selfless; they just expand their understanding of self to be much more encompassing than it is for most of us. To be sure, the expansiveness of the concerns that a sage—and even an exemplary person—takes to be relevant to themselves means that they will balance the various goods in life rather differently than many of us do. Confucian sages are more balanced than a selfless "moral saint," but still are very aware of their connections and responsibilities to the rest of the world.

The final sense of continuity is the continuity of ethical demands. Zhu Xi criticizes those who have "the attitude that they are already good enough": in fact, there are always more things that one can be attentive to, more ways that one can try to do better.[13] As one modern scholar puts it, "The rare possibility of perfection is real for Xunzi. This possibility serves to chasten the virtuous to remain dissatisfied with themselves and continue striving to enact the Way flawlessly, not just well."[14] Think again here of "life-long worries." We should not think that ethical continuity is only a "demand," though. It is also an encouragement, emphasizing that even doing a little bit better is still an important accomplishment, a way of taking another step on the path toward sagehood, and that we should feel good about these small bits of progress.

The Confucian model of linked stages of improvement therefore helps to put the lofty goal of sagehood into perspective. Indeed, the same scholar I just quoted also notes that "moral formation may rest on rather different sorts of virtues, reflecting different stages in this ongoing process, so that looking only at perfected virtue would miss much of importance."[15] The work one must do as one matures ethically is partly distinct from the goal at which one is ultimately aiming. For example, sagehood is not, ultimately, about having memorized large swaths of classical texts. But a concerted effort to read in the ways that Zhu Xi recommends is nonetheless part of the—or at least a—path to sagehood. Similarly, many Confucian texts offer up good-but-not-perfect role models for us to emulate; in some ways it may be easier to learn from these "worthies" than from sages.[16]

The idea of continuous stages of improvement can also help us to figure out what to make of Liang Shuming, the self-proclaimed Sage with whom this chapter began. It seems that Liang was determined to become a sage all at once—to force himself to never err—but that the result of skipping steps of development was lots of gritting of teeth and not much spontaneity. In the terms of Chapter 13, Liang had to "fake it" a lot. As we saw there, faking is almost always part of moral growth. But too much faking can be self-undermining. The contemporary philosopher Christine Swanton has argued that "we should not be virtuous beyond our strength."[17] If we try something that we are not ready for, we may well fail, undermining our own confidence and letting down others. This fits well with a view we find in *Mengzi*: "Wisdom is like skill, while sagehood is like strength. It is like shooting from beyond a hundred paces. It is due to your strength that the arrow reaches the target, but it is not due to your strength that it hits its mark."[18] The "strength" that Swanton and Mengzi are talking about is not force of will, but rather the development of one's moral faculties as a whole: the maturing of one's level of commitment and the expansion of one's sense of self. One should always be working to progress (to get "stronger"), and some faking it is needed, but Liang's humorless determination to be perfect is not a good model for us.

* * *

My emphasis so far on the continuity between sages and us may be giving you the impression that sagehood is no big deal. This risks making sagehood sound accessible at the cost of losing its significance. Is this all there is to the central ideal of Confucianism? What about the idea of "enlightenment" that features in so many traditions?

The example of sagely behavior that I have most often referred to is probably Shun's interactions with his family. What did he do? From one perspective, it can seem perfectly ordinary: he genuinely loved his brother and parents and he treated them the way that one treats beloved relatives. On the other hand, let's not forget that the brother and parents in question were selfish and power-hungry, to the point that they repeatedly tried to kill Shun! Shun's continued love for them is thus anything but ordinary. So deeply committed is he to their flourishing and eventual moral growth that he continues to love and embrace them, even putting his brother on the throne of You Bi (admittedly without any actual power).

Confucians regularly connect sagely attitudes and behavior like this with enlightenment, but they treat the experience of enlightenment with considerable subtlety. (In fact, this is an area in which there was real debate among Neo-Confucians; the view I present here is the most influential, mainstream view, but there are outliers.[19]) One may experience sudden moments of clarity in which one sees-and-feels interconnections far beyond the norm, and they may indicate moral growth, but they do not signal the arrival of a new, lasting state of consciousness. Such enlightenment experiences can help one to glimpse the expansive sense of self that Confucian cultivation aims to realize. As one gets closer to sagehood, one should more thoroughly attain the "unimpeded interconnection" mentioned in Chapter 11. Again, though, this is not a fundamentally different state of consciousness from the one you now occupy. After all, we all manage some degree of reverence, commitment, and spontaneous responsiveness some of the time, in easy cases at least. Moments of at least partial enlightenment—when you feel that at least for right now, everything fits together and makes sense—point toward what is possible all the time for a sage.

With all these considerations in mind, it would make sense if you were asking whether sagehood is really possible. Can someone be perfect, responding with ease and appropriateness to every situation they encounter? There are two dimensions to this challenge. On the one hand, you might wonder whether anyone can really manage the extraordinary feats that sages supposedly do: Could anyone really love his brother when put in Shun's shoes? On the other hand, you might be skeptical about the consistency with which sages are said to pull this off. They never falter? That seems unhuman.

Let's start with the first dimension. Perhaps you have a relative who is frustratingly selfish, whose inability to see things from other' perspectives and rigidity about their preferences causes strife within your family. Can you see your way to continuing to include them, embrace their good qualities, love them—in the hope that they will grow into a more generous and flexible person? It can be challenging, and may require some "faking," but this is something that most of us can do. This is not as extreme as Shun, but the basic psychology is the same. If most of us can love an annoying relative, surely some of us could even love a murderous one.

The second dimension has to do with consistency, and this exact concern has been raised by the philosopher Owen Flanagan in a book about what forms of morality are "psychologically realistic." Flanagan poses himself the following question: If we are aware of people who have responded perfectly to certain situations, even under considerable duress, why cannot we imagine people who do this all the time? He has two related answers. One is that even if we can imagine such morally perfect responses to particular situations, it is much harder to imagine the underlying morally perfect character that would have to be in place for a true sage. Second, he queries whether a person can keep up his or her "moral guard" over the course of a whole life: "There are too many other things besides morality that need attending to, and being perfect is tiring after a while."[20]

Flanagan himself admits that neither of these considerations is completely conclusive. Being on one's "moral guard" sounds a lot like Liang Shuming, and a genuine sage has undergone a deeper transformation than it appears that Liang ever did. I think that the continuity of stages of moral growth also helps answer Flanagan's questions. Surely we can imagine how a "petty person" might grow into a "committed scholar," and it doesn't seem so hard to envision such a learner maturing into a "exemplary person." Why not the final step, then? There is no obvious barrier, and I submit that that is enough for a Confucian's practical purpose. We can aim at sagehood, understanding that what this means is aiming to be better than we are now, in all the ways that sages are better than we are now. That is enough ambition for a lifetime.

16 | DEATH

One of the greatest tragedies of the COVID-19 pandemic was the frequency with which elderly people were stricken and died while cut off from their families by the necessities of quarantines. Medical professionals the world over were heroic, both in their efforts to save lives and to ease the passing of those who succumbed to the virus, but there is still something devastating in the images of children unable to share in their parents' final moments. Does Confucianism have any special insight to help us to understand the difficult yet ubiquitous subject of death?

Compared to many religions and, for that matter, much of Western philosophy, Confucianism might be thought to downplay the significance of our deaths. An oft-quoted passage in the *Analects* runs as follows:

> Ji Lu asked about serving ghosts and spirits. The Master said, "You are not yet able to serve people; how could you be able to serve ghosts and spirits?" Ji Lu added, "I venture to ask

about death?" The Master replied, "You do not yet understand life; how could you understand death?"[1]

Is Kongzi saying that death ultimately isn't that important? Not
at all, though the Confucian attitude toward death is indeed
quite different from what many readers will be used to. Once we
have understood what Kongzi has in mind, we'll come to see that
Confucians offer a comforting and profound way to think about
the roles that deaths play in our lives.

To understand how distinctive the Confucian stance is, let's
begin with a glance at some alternatives. Plato believed that philosophy was actually "training for death":

> It really has been shown to us that, if we are ever to have pure
> knowledge, we must escape from the body and observe things
> in themselves with the soul by itself. It seems likely that we
> shall, only then, when we are dead, attain that which we de-
> sire and of which we claim to be lovers, namely, wisdom.[2]

Philosophers should therefore fear death least of all people.
For many Christians, their faith in an afterlife similarly leads to
discounting the loss involved in their own death. Freud, in contrast, argues that these views are forms of denial; as one scholar puts
it, "the threat of death is so overwhelming to our individual egos
that it moves us to work mightily to deceive ourselves and banish
the obvious fact of death from consciousness."[3] Existentialists base
their philosophy on accepting the fact of our impending death—
that is, our mortality—and believe that the only authentic existence embraces our finiteness.[4] In all of these cases, the fact of

one's own, individual death is central to how human existence is conceived.

For Confucians, what matters is to live one's life well in relationship with others. Sometimes, tragedy intervenes and a life is cut short, leaving others bereft. In certain extreme circumstances, living well might involve sacrificing one's life. Most people's deaths, though, come at the end of a normal span in which they have had ample opportunities to live rich, committed, and connected lives. It is important to mourn the loss of our loved ones, but then gradually move on with our own lives. As we will see, Confucians put more emphasis on the deaths of others than on one's own mortality.

* * *

Kongzi's statement to Ji Lu, "You do not yet understand life; how could you understand death?," is often taken as an evasion or even a suggestion that knowledge of "death" is a kind of secret, reserved for initiates only. At least for those of us familiar with ideas of afterlife or reincarnation, it's tempting to think that Ji Lu had something like this in mind, and Kongzi cleverly changes the subject. Certainly there were various beliefs about post-death survival in early China, as suggested by clues like documents and other objects found in tombs.[5] But from what we can see in sources like the *Analects*, these beliefs did not play significant roles in Confucian thinking. As P.J. Ivanhoe puts it, if Kongzi "believed in some form of post-life survival, this was not embedded in a greater web of beliefs about a final judgment, subsequent punishment and reward, or any notion of reincarnation."[6] Instead, Ivanhoe argues that Kongzi means what he says in quite a straight-forward way: in order to know the significance of someone's death, one has to understand what it is to live a good life. The way that we should think about someone dying is connected to how they lived. This means that there are only three legitimate Confucian questions about death: about sacrifice, about tragedy, and about normal grief and mourning.

Let's begin with sacrifice. When might it be appropriate to sacrifice one's life? Kongzi describes exemplary people as "loving learning with firm confidence and perfecting the excellence of the Way even unto death."[7] In case the meaning of "even unto death" isn't clear, elsewhere he says:

> The committed scholar and the humane person will not seek to live at the expense of injuring their humaneness. They will even sacrifice their lives to preserve their humaneness complete.[8]

For his part, Mengzi agrees, stating:

> I like eating fish, and I also like eating bear's paw. If I cannot have the two together, I will let the fish go, and take the bear's paw. So, I like life, and I also like righteousness. If I cannot keep the two together, I will let life go, and choose righteousness.[9]

In one sense, Mengzi's statement might be a bit misleading. The point isn't merely that one prefers righteousness to life as one might prefer chocolate to vanilla, but that one is *committed* to humaneness and righteousness such that when it is impossible to maintain them while living, one chooses death. As we know, commitments are life-long undertakings that gradually mature, ultimately aiming at a sincere, unified, integrated personality that manifests spontaneously, without the need for striving or control.

Back in Chapter 11 we met a small business owner who was forced to lay off workers owing to "fate"—that is, a circumstance outside her control (a poor economy). In the *Analects*, Kongzi praises two early princes who were faced with an even graver fate: the fall of their dynasty. Their commitments led them to refuse to eat food now associated with the usurpers, resulting in their starving to death.[10] Other examples of such principled deaths can be found throughout Chinese history. The idea is not that life is undervalued, but that what we should seek is a good life, a life of ethical commitment. Part and parcel of living such a good life is one's willingness to relinquish one's life if necessary to retain one's commitment. Of course, deaths like those of the two princes are also occasions for sadness, but because of the ways in which their deaths exemplify the depth of their commitments, we remember such lives as well-lived. Kongzi emphasizes that the two princes are still celebrated, while others who profited from collaboration with the usurpers are long forgotten.

Cases of tragic death are like sacrifices in that lives end early, but unlike sacrifices there is nothing positive to take away from such fates. The *Analects* describes Kongzi's reactions when young students die not from heroic sacrifice, but from arbitrary illness. As Bo Niu lies dying, Kongzi wails, "Our losing him is due to fate! That such a man should have such a sickness! That such a man should have such a sickness!"[11] The Master's reaction to Yan Hui's death is even more severe: "Alas! Heaven is destroying me! Heaven is destroying me!"[12] In these cases, fate (or Heaven) is not just something to be borne, but to be railed against. Mengzi helps us to understand what is going on when he says that dying as a result of exhaustively following the Way can be a "proper fate," whereas dying as a criminal is no one's "proper fate."[13] Being cut down by disease while in one's prime is similarly not a proper fate—all the more so because one committed no crime. As Ivanhoe points out, the randomness of such an "improper fate" is disturbing even to highly cultivated people; it unsettles any confidence that we may find harmony in our world.[14]

Remember, though, that "fate"—or what is the same thing, the unseen results of "Heaven"—is not the conscious plan of a supernatural intelligence. Unlike those whose view of the cosmos revolves around a single, all-powerful, and benevolent deity, Confucians do not have to ask how a tragic death can be part of "the plan." There is no plan. There is simply the continuous process of change which has at its heart the production of life, and which Confucians see as capable of harmony. Individual lives are finite, and so the process of change involves death and destruction, some of which happens too soon. What infuriates us about tragic death is the sense of unexpected, unmitigated loss. Our own lives are now bereft of the rich possibilities for living together—parent and child, wife and husband, or (in Kongzi's case) teacher and student—that would have provided so much meaning and value. In the moment, the sense of loss can be so piercing that we feel "destroyed." Even so, the counsel Confucians give us in such circumstances is not fundamentally different from their teachings regarding deaths more generally: grieve properly and then gradually get back to your life.

In Kongzi's concise formulation, "Mourning should reach to grief and then stop."[15]

Most of us have never stopped to think about why we mourn the way we do. As I acknowledged at the very beginning of this book, even amidst my tears during the days after my father's passing, the philosopher in me was seeking a better understanding. In light of what I have already said about sacrificial and tragic deaths, we might expect Confucians to be rather blasé about someone who had lived out a full and good life, but to the contrary they insist that the death of one's parent demands the most sustained mourning. While drafting this chapter I commiserated with a close friend whose father had just died of COVID-19 at the age of ninety-four after a life of love and accomplishment. Far from being at peace, her grief was mixed with anger that this had happened only weeks before he would have received a vaccine. Everyone's story is unique, but the death of a parent often hits us hard. Why is this so?

The death of anyone you know ruptures the network of relationships that helps to define who you are. When you share experiences, values, and even tensions with others this gives significance to your actions—and so when someone is gone, it is as if part of yourself has been lost as well. Never again can you share a tea with her or argue with him. Parents play a special role in this network of relationships. This is clear in Confucian philosophy, particularly in the importance it places on filial piety, and it is clear in our own lives. For almost all of us, it is in our relationship with our parent or parents that we began to grow as social, moral beings. Confucians therefore insist that a child's attitude toward his or her parents is the vital "root" from which goodness will grow. The love and respect for parents that is called "filial piety" is something that should grow and change over a lifetime, as both you and your parents age. The result is the unique species of loss that you experience when one of them dies. As Amy Olberding has put it, the Confucians enjoin us to lead our lives in ways that promote grief upon the passing of a parent.[16] Because they are so special to us, our grief is so acute.

Grieving is thus a necessary kind of pain—pain that reflects the "loss of self" that death signifies.[17] But too much or too prolonged pain is not a good thing. The death of someone close to you will change you but it should not leave you traumatized, permanently unable to cope. The point of structured processes of mourning is to enable us to manage our losses. With help from other contemporary scholars of Confucianism, we can identify both short-term and long-term strategies by which Confucian mourning rituals aim to help us.

Short-term approaches aim to "guard" the bereaved against the excessive trauma that might cause them to lose their way. This works best when mourning is public: sharing someone's sorrow (as opposed to saying "it will be fine") guards them from isolation. Similarly, the rituals of one's tradition serve as "orienting landmarks" that help one navigate when all seems overwhelming and unfamiliar.[18] I well remember the ways that traditional liturgy in the church my father had long attended felt right, even to a nonbeliever like me. And strategically placed boxes of tissues were a clear sign that open expressions of sorrow were expected and fine. It is even possible that the many details of mourning rituals guard us in another way: drawing on psychological research, one scholar suggests that "focusing on ritualized prescriptive behavior can help flood the working memory and prevent potentially hazardous thoughts."[19]

At the same time that mourning rituals are serving their short-term functions, they are laying the foundation for longer-term well-being. Dictionary definitions of "mourning" speak of sorrow and ritual but are silent about celebration, which nonetheless seems to be a part of many cultures' ways of mourning, from somber eulogies to lively wakes. Celebration of the deceased's life helps each of the bereaved to begin to reweave the narrative fabric of their selves, now including the deceased as an "ancestor" (to use Confucian terminology). Even after official mourning is over, the regular practice of ancestral rites in Confucian and other cultures reinforces the ability of the deceased to live on in a different fashion. In the words of one scholar, such rites "replace the memory of the loss of one's parents with the life-affirming celebration of their life."[20]

* * *

Not everyone is convinced that the attitude toward death that I've been describing is sufficient to our needs. The eminent scholar of contemporary Chinese religions, Yang Fenggang, believes that Confucianism's religiosity is too "thin" to fully serve the needs to Chinese people today.[21] Yang, who himself is Christian, believes that Confucianism can contribute toward a Chinese "civil religion" but says that Confucianism is not a "full religion" and has trouble establishing its "sacredness."[22] These are obviously complicated matters but a main reason for the limited role Yang assigns to Confucianism is its failure to discuss existential questions surrounding death, such as whether one can somehow transcend death.

One way to answer Yang's concern is by pointing out that within the long Confucian tradition, there are in fact some theorists who have sought to "understand death" in the existential way Yang is seeking. To be sure, most Neo-Confucians like Zhu Xi and Wang Yangming follow the lead of Kongzi when it comes to the question of death. Their context is different because Buddhist views related to reincarnation are now widespread in China. (Buddhism in China has many sects. The adherents of some aspire to be reborn in the Western Paradise; others seek the cessation of the cycle of rebirth.) Still, Zhu Xi channels Kongzi: "Someone talked about cultivating an afterlife, and Master Zhu said: You don't cultivate this life, but you cultivate the next life—what sense does that make?"[23] There were other Neo-Confucians, though, who reacted differently to the Buddhist insistence that one's death (or rebirth) was of great philosophical consequence. For a thinker like Wang Ji (1498–1583 CE), "If one cannot explore, and come to understand the fundamental causes of life and death, then even brilliant work, outstanding talent, and the most successful career will in an instant turn into empty trappings when death comes upon one."[24]

So, is it fair to say that a deep exploration of death is lacking in mainstream Confucianism? Each reader needs to decide that individually, but in my judgment, Confucianism's approach is profound. From the perspective of the sum total of our experiences in the ever-changing cosmos, Kongzi and his heirs see that it is our lives together that matter. This assertion is not a denial of death; it's a specific, and, for many, helpful way to think about and respond to it. Death is a deep and troubling fact, to be sure, but it is troubling for those who live on, not for the deceased.[25]

Part Four

Challenges and the Future

Challenges and the Future

17 | PROGRESSIVE CONFUCIANISM

A few years ago, I was interviewed by a Chinese journalist. She asked about what I was calling "progressive Confucianism" (prompted by a book of mine that had just come out in Chinese), but she was clearly rather skeptical.[1] I had the sense that she felt she knew what Confucianism was and she wasn't interested in *that*. So, this foreigner talking about something different, which he also called Confucianism, was mainly a curiosity. By the end of the conversation, though, she was genuinely intrigued, realizing that maybe she had been wrong about Confucianism—which, admittedly, as a communications major in college she had never really studied.

The journalist's initial negative view of Confucianism was not a coincidence. Over the last century many have been critical of Confucianism, seeing it as the defender of feudalism, hierarchy, and patriarchy. Politicians and ideologues in more than one East Asian country have attempted to use it to justify authoritarian government. More generally, people have often seen it as hopelessly out of step with modernity, relying on mystical or metaphysical ideas that have no place in a scientific worldview. Some "cultural conservatives" have embraced precisely these ideas and called for Confucianism to become a state religion, but this has just served to confirm for the majority that Confucianism is neither progressive nor relevant.

To take Confucianism seriously as a potentially progressive way of life, it's vital that we face these sorts of negative images head-on. Before turning to issues like gender, hierarchy, and the prospects for Confucianism in a pluralistic world, let me first set the stage by addressing the following, more preliminary questions:

1. Is it legitimate to draw, willy-nilly, on the disparate range of Confucian thinkers that I have? What about differences among these philosophers?
2. Does the focus on living a Confucian life downplay the role of textual scholarship that really should lie at the core of what it is to be a Confucian?
3. Does approaching Confucianism as a guide to living a good life flatten it out or "disenchant" the Confucian tradition in a way that drains it of meaning?
4. If Confucianism is taken in an inclusive direction, instead of being as elitist as it was historically, do we lose its most valuable insights?
5. Is this just a hodge-podge of Western ideas dressed up in Chinese clothing?

* * *

Confucianism is an evolving tradition, and like earlier moments in the tradition, modern Confucianism both builds on and critiques what has come before. This is just what living traditions do. Many analysts have stressed that genuine traditions are characterized by internal diversity and rational (in the tradition's own terms) debate aimed at "carrying its enquiries forward."[2] And there is ample evidence that modern Confucians are engaged in just such a project. As one of the most influential 20th-century Confucians, Feng Youlan (1895–1990 CE) put it, modern Confucians can and must "continue" the tradition rather than just "follow" it.[3] "Following" past versions of the tradition would mean rigidly adhering to interpretations of the tradition from hundreds or even thousands of years ago. This kind of fetishizing of the past is almost always driven by extremist and ideological contemporary motives and is also based on the false ideas that some earlier iteration of the tradition was pure, while more recent versions are mere interpretations; and that we have unmitigated access to this earlier, pure moment. Like many other traditions, Confucianism today has its "fundamentalists," but their claims to be able to speak for an original Confucianism are deeply problematic.[4]

There is another kind of "following": this is the work of the historian, who strives to follow and describe the ideas of past thinkers without casting any judgment on the aptness of those ideas to present-day life. (That may well have been what Feng actually had in mind by his mention of "following.") Modern "continuations" of a tradition need to be based on good, historical understandings of the tradition's past—lest the modern so-called continuation be invented out of whole cloth—but the modern continuation need not be limited to one or another of the specific earlier voices. Although I have emphasized similarities much more than differences, all Confucians had differences with one another. Sometimes these are differences of emphasis and some-times more substantive disagreements. What I am doing here is synthesizing the best ideas within the tradition in keeping with its core commitments.

How do we know what these core commitments are, and how do we judge whether a modern claim is sufficiently based on the past? Where some traditions have priests, Confucianism has *shi*. *Shi* (which can be singular or plural) is a tricky term to translate. In this book I have used "scholars" (as in "committed scholars," one of the stages of moral development discussed earlier); others have used "literati" or "gentlemen," each of which captures some of its flavor. Certainly *shi* are concerned with the textual tradition of Confucianism. They study and comment on this ever-growing body of insights, stories, and abstruse explanations. But *shi* need not be professional academics. Indeed, they are not only scholars; *shi* are committed to learning in its full sense of learning to be an ever-better person—just as you may be, yourself. If we understand "phi-losopher" in its original Greek sense, as a lover of wisdom seeking to understand and live the best life, then it's quite appropriate to trans-late *shi* as philosopher. At any rate, it is the community of *shi* who debate and strive to decide what to make of Confucianism today. One doesn't have to be (or aspire to be) a *shi* to live a Confucian life or to learn from Confucianism, but as we'll see later, these days the *shi* are an increasingly diverse and international group.

* * *

Religion and metaphysics have a lot in common. Both seek to offer deep, non-obvious explanations for the way the world is and the way it should be. Both have long been out of favor among those who feel that science provides all the explanation we need or can get; the early sociologist Max Weber (1864–1920 CE) termed this the "disenchantment of the world."[5] Of course, religion has not gone away, and even many atheists feel that there are profound truths about our relation to one another—or to non-human animals, or to the environment—that cannot be captured by physics or biology. A central part of modern philosophy, including modern Confucianism, has been to try to understand such metaphysical possibilities.

My goal here has not been to settle such issues, but rather to suggest the ways in which the various stances that Confucians have adopted might speak to how we live today. In some cases, such as the contention that we humans have a positive orientation to the world built into us, it is possible to find certain kinds of scientific support, as we saw briefly in Chapter 5. Even here, though, Confucian claims far outrun what our science can yet speak to. It is one thing to say that rudimentary positive responses to others may be natural (the "sprouts"); quite another to say that the world (or even "cosmos") as a whole is value-laden, with emergent possibilities for harmony all around us. And yet is it so hard to imagine that our world is in a continual process of life-generating, patterned change? That we can identify our part in these complex interactions, and in so doing help to more fully realize the latent harmony?

Perhaps you do find that hard to imagine—or at least, to take seriously. Very little that I have said here depends on following the Confucians along the path of their metaphysical (or spiritual, or religious—call it what you will) thinking. Some contemporary fans of Confucianism find the classical thinkers to be less profligate in their metaphysics than the Neo-Confucians, and so build their modern views only on the more ancient foundations. Others, in my experience, find that Neo-Confucian discussions of Pattern and cosmic harmony speak strongly to them. I have tried to craft this book in a way that emphasizes what Confucians share in common, while also allowing some of their diverse perspectives to appear and to tempt those who are interested.[6]

* * *

In several chapters we have seen that modern Confucians endorse the idea that their teachings should be aimed at everyone. But didn't Confucians throughout their history actually teach primarily to literate men, especially those with the leisure to study? More worryingly, mightn't it be the case that Confucian insights depend on a kind of elitism? After all, there are a number of theorists today in China who claim Confucian roots for their contemporary theories of meritocratic—as opposed to democratic—government.[7] If we jettison elitism, do we lose something essential?

There is a great deal of nuance to the arguments among Confucian political philosophers that is impossible to capture here in a few short sentences.[8] One thing is clear: even the earliest Confucians believed that all people have equal moral potential. This was an important shift from earlier beliefs in hereditary privilege.[9] As Mengzi puts it, the great sages Yao and Shun "were the same as other people," which affirms that "everyone can become a Yao or a Shun."[10] It is also clear that this belief in natural equality coexisted with hierarchical political and social structures. No Confucian before the modern era ever envisioned an alternative to monarchy.

In my judgment, the best explanation for this situation was articulated a few years ago in a PhD dissertation by a student at the University of Hong Kong, Elton Chan. Chan makes a distinction between "ideal theories" (which describe the best possible outcomes) and "non-ideal theories" (which are more practical compromises, though still aiming toward the ideals in the long run). The problem for Confucians, Chan argues, is that their hierarchical non-ideal theory evolved in such a way that it became detached from the ideal. The institutions that Confucians built and supported had the effect of excluding large numbers of people from a genuine chance at moral growth. The result was a "permanent second-best."[11] Chan therefore argues that to have a realistic shot at achieving their ideals, Confucians today need to renovate their non-ideal theory to be inclusive and participatory. In effect, what this means is that Confucians need to embrace some form of democracy.

The key point here is that we can distinguish between the deep commitments of Confucianism and the various means that have historically been tried in order to realize those commitments. The fundamental moral equality of all people is a deep commitment. The vision of ethical growth and of good lives in community with others that I have sketched in this book should apply to everyone. And in fact, inclusion and openness are important for another, equally deep reason. The Confucian ideal of harmony means finding ways that differences complement each other, contributing to a greater whole. To achieve this one must learn from others' perspectives rather than insisting only on one's own. As you'll recall, one important Confucian lesson speaks directly to this theme: we saw that for music to unite and shape us, it must be sufficiently open and inclusive to speak to the diverse members of contemporary communities. As our communities change and the traditions on which "we" draw multiply, so must our music develop. Conserving our deep values means being open to change in our specific practices.

* * *

A common reaction of self-styled conservative Confucians to more progressive approaches to the tradition is to insist that progressive Confucianism isn't Confucian at all but is really just "liberalism" or "Western thought."[12] The mere fact that Confucians like myself are reading and learning from other schools of thought (including liberalism and feminism) cannot mean that our writings are not Confucian, though, because this has been true from the beginning. Mengzi and Xunzi learned from Mohists and Daoists. Zhu Xi and Wang Yangming learned from Buddhists. Twentieth-century "New Confucians" like Mou Zongsan (1909–1995 CE) learned from Kant and Hegel. No thinker operates in a vacuum, and this has always been the case. Throughout, the tradition was being "conserved" by being developed in conversation with other ideas and other experiences. Mou Zongsan himself put it this way: "If one is without a firm commitment to life, penetrating wisdom, and pervasive ethics, then one cannot speak of 'conserving.' True conserving is concretely embedded in the practice of creativity: the two are not opposed."[13] In other words, insofar as we "conserve" the virtuous characteristics and affirmation of life that the tradition has shown us to be vital, we are thereby progressing—both growing ethically and making things better in our world.

The idea that ethical insight leads to progressive political change, which in turn leads to greater realization of our potential for virtue, lies at the heart of progressive Confucianism. The institutions advocated by progressive Confucians are valued not because of their ancient pedigree but because of their capacity to assist in the realization of the fundamental human virtues that Confucians have valued since ancient times. Social structures that set barriers to the realization of virtue, therefore, need to be critiqued and changed. Progressive Confucian criticism of social, economic, or political oppression will often resemble the criticisms raised by other sorts of progressivism, but progressive Confucianism remains true to its founding insights in many ways.

This book's focus is on how you, living in the modern day, can live a Confucian life. One part of that will be advocating for certain kinds of broader change, but socio-political engagement is only one aspect of living as a Confucian. Questions of public policy and political authority therefore take a backseat in this book to more personal aspects of our lived realities. I and others have written extensively elsewhere on progressive Confucian socio-political ideas. As part of our exploration of Confucianism as a guide to a good life, it's important to understand a few of the ways in which modern Confucianism must interact critically and productively with movements like feminism and liberalism—but without losing its right to call itself Confucianism.

18 | GENDER

Decades ago, the influential modern Confucian Tu Wei-ming identified feminism's critique as the single greatest challenge to the possibility of a viable Confucianism. The problem is not just that historical Confucian societies were strongly patriarchal, but also that Confucian philosophy can seem to provide theoretical support for gender inequality, and furthermore that some Confucians today continue to explicitly embrace patriarchy. Jiang Qing, an outspoken, conservative Confucian published an interview a few years ago called "Only Confucians Can Make a Place for Modern Women": his theme is that women will be better off if they return to their "natural" places within the household.[1] It is no wonder that many contemporary East Asians think that "Confucian feminism" is an oxymoron.

Who is right? The core ideas related to gender and social roles within Confucianism allow for multiple possibilities, but when these ideas are combined with other key Confucian commitments (that we have already met), it becomes clear that Confucians today should embrace an egalitarian conception of gender. This does not mean viewing everyone as simply the same, however; Confucian ideas help us to shape relationships and societies that honor both equality and difference.

* * *

Let's begin with a brief look at one of China's most ancient classics, the *Book of Changes* (or *Yi Jing* / *I Ching*). What started out as a text used for divination gradually transformed, as layers of commentary and interpretation were added, into a broad framework for understanding basic features of the cosmos. The *Changes* is common property to China's indigenous philosophical traditions, very much including Confucianism. At its heart lie the twin ideas of *yin* and *yang*, which in turn become central to Chinese and Confucian ideas of gender. Each of the *Changes*'s sixty-four hexagrams is made up of a series of six lines, either broken or unbroken, respectively representing *yin* and *yang*. The basic idea of the text is that the cosmos can be understood as an ongoing series of patterned, interlocking transformations. Large changes (a marriage, a royal abdication, a drought) are formed by nested, smaller changes, and also ramify into various other changes. All these changes can be abstractly represented as patterns of *yin* and *yang*.

What are *yin* and *yang*? Their earliest meanings are the shady and sunny sides of a hill. In other words, from the beginning *yin* and *yang* are both linked and dynamic: as the sun moves through the sky, the sizes and locations of the shady side (*yin*) and the sunny side (*yang*) change in corresponding ways. Understanding the rhythmic changes to the world was of course very important in a largely agricultural society, and over time the basic ideas of *yin* and *yang* acquired a series of associations: *yin* with darkness, rest, stillness, receptivity; *yang* with light, activity, movement, action. Looked at this way, *yin* and *yang* are equally valuable: no activity without rest, no productive action without receptivity (think of speaking without listening: what good is that?), and so on. In other words, the earliest uses of *yin* and *yang* were non-hierarchical and, not coincidentally, not linked to gender. As *yin* and *yang* increasingly became central theoretical concepts, though, they were applied to more and more areas of life, including to the distinction between men and women.[2]

It would have been possible to use *yin* and *yang* to understand gender differences in a non-hierarchical and non-fixed way. For example, suppose that *yang* is associated with things like aggressiveness and extroversion and *yin* with creativity and introversion. However exactly these traits are in turn linked to gender, we might recognize that both sets of characteristics are important—some more so in some contexts than others—and also that people display changing sets of characteristics over time. In addition, people routinely display "mixed" sets of characteristics, such as creativity and extroversion. (The *Changes*, with its hexagrams made up of many different combinations of *yin* and *yang* lines, would of course have expected nothing else.) Not only would this ground an egalitarian way of looking at gender differences, but even contemporary ideas of non-binary gender and gender fluidity could easily be accommodated in such a framework.

This did not happen.[3] Instead, by the time Confucianism had become fully intertwined with imperial ideology in the mid-Han

Dynasty (1st c. BCE), *yin* has a firm association with women and femininity and *yang* with men and masculinity (no distinction is drawn between biological sex and socially constructed gender). *Yang* and males (and rulers) are seen as hierarchically superior to *yin* and women (and subjects). Furthermore, the idea that women and men have distinct realms has also taken root: the "inner" for women and the "outer" for men. Scholars have offered a variety of explanations, both sociological and philosophical, for why the associations among female, *yin*, and the inner realm become so rigid, but these issues need not detain us here.

It is certainly relevant that—as apologists have insisted and critics have generally acknowledged—Confucian ideas of gender are not based on a "strong binary" division between males and females. As we have seen, the underlying *yin-yang* theory is perfectly compatible with some ambiguity, which may be part of the explanation for the relative acceptance of homosexuality in Chinese culture (at least for men, and at least as long as they also marry a woman).[4] In addition, in theory the relationship between men and women is not one of domination and submission, but rather of complementarity: different, mutually supportive activities, with men and women both having authority in their respective realms. And where the line gets drawn between "inner" and "outer" can also be flexible and negotiable, depending on the context.[5]

Still, the distinction between men and women is clear and emphasized; indeed, according to many Confucian texts, "distinction" becomes the defining characteristic of the relationship between men and women. It is true that there are well-known texts collecting stories of the lives of exemplary women and educational texts that teach women to be virtuous. But for the most part, and increasingly over time, the qualities these texts called for were quite different from those of a virtuous man. One authoritative text describes "women's virtue" in this way:

> Exhibit tranquility, unhurried composure, chastity, and quietude. Safeguard the integrity of regulations. Keep things in an orderly manner. Guard one's action with a sense of shame. In movement and rest, it is always done in proper measure.[6]

These qualities are not entirely unrelated to the canonical Confucian virtues we met in earlier chapters, but their scope is dramatically narrower. For most later Confucian commentators on women's education—the vast majority of whom are men—in fact, it is a simple truth that women cannot become "sages." The gates to the highest realms of moral achievement are barred. There are a few, partial exceptions, as we will shortly see, but even so it is difficult to view traditional Confucianism as anything other than anti-feminist.

* * *

Of course, endorsement of patriarchy does not distinguish premodern Confucianism from most other religions and philosophical traditions around the world. Buddhists have applauded celibate monks and derided lustful women, Aristotle held that women were "natural slaves," and Christians have insisted on male authority.[7] Feminist movements are primarily modern phenomena, in part because of social changes that economic and technological developments have catalyzed. Often these movements have been explicitly understood as anti-traditional; but more recently scholars and activists alike have begun to see that the distinctive current paths of diverse feminist movements around the world, and also their possible futures, are shaped in part by underlying traditions. In addition, when we look back at historical traditions, we can often discover discordant voices within them: critics who saw, even prior to the great changes of modernity, some of the problems or prejudices associated with patriarchy. In this spirit, let us consider three more egalitarian stances that some Confucians have historically adopted, and on this foundation build an argument for Confucian gender equality.

The first position for us to examine is "separate but equal." Most historical Confucians believed that the abilities, virtues, and spheres of activity of men and women were separate and *unequal*. Women had their sphere of activity and virtues for which they could strive, but these were explicitly understood to be lesser in scope and value than the corresponding ideals that applied to men. For at least a few Confucian thinkers, though, this did not sit right. Like all Confucians, the 16th-century Neo-Confucian Luo Rufang (1515–1588 CE) believed that filial piety was extremely important. But Luo observes that the affection and care of mothers for their children plays an even more fundamental role than filial piety, as it elicits filial piety of the best kind. Luo believes that filial piety arises out of a sense of gratitude and appreciation for the unsolicited love and sacrifices of the parents, and the truest filial piety therefore blooms in the hearts of those who have been cared for most wholeheartedly. "Maternal affection" is the paradigm for such care. Nurturance as well as social and moral education primarily took place within the household, under the supervision of one's mother. Exemplary mothers are thus of the greatest significance to the world. Luo still reserves the term "sage" for men, but Luo strongly suggests that "sages" are not the only kind of moral paragon; it can be argued that Luo saw exemplary women as meeting greater moral demands, and thus as achieving greater moral distinction, than sages.[8]

Luo's appreciation of the central role played in his society by loving mothers is commendable, but of course my choosing to label this position "separate but equal"—the phrase used in a notorious 1896 US Supreme Court decision endorsing racial segregation—suggests that we should not be content with Luo's position. Luo says that women's love and sacrifice are enormously valuable, but he both closes off these forms of virtue from men and does not even consider the possibility that women might thrive living other kinds of lives. Strikingly, this sharp distinction between gender roles is echoed in the contemporary meanings of the English terms "to father" and "to mother." But surely other ways of thinking about child-rearing are possible? Thanks to my university's generous parental leave policy, I was able to stay home with each of our children for several months after my wife returned to work. These experiences had deep effects on me; for one sign of the effects they had on our children, consider that our eldest called both my wife and me "MommyDaddy" for quite a while!

For something closer to true equality than Luo Rufang has to offer, we need to turn to a different traditional author, the late-14th-century Empress Renxiaowen (1362–1407 CE). The empress authored a text called *Teachings for the Inner Court* that aims to instruct young women, particularly those aspiring to a role in the palace, how to cultivate their characters and manage their behavior.

Unlike almost all male authors, the empress is unambiguous that women have the same nature and can develop the same virtues as men; women can be sages. Where Luo Rufang emphasized the distinctively feminine virtue of maternal affection, Empress Renxiaowen often refers to standard Confucian virtues like humaneness and righteousness. At one point, she imagines someone responding to her by saying, "This is the sages' way of exhibiting filial piety; it is not suitable for women." The empress replies: "Filial piety is part of heavenly endowed nature. How can there be difference here between a man and a woman? In serving one's parents, one ought to follow the supreme models of the sages."[9]

Still, even if women's natures are the same as men's and sagehood is also open to them, Empress Renxiaowen envisions a woman's role as different from a man's. It is via her role as an "inner helpmate" that a woman can play her part, educating children and supporting her husband; even though this may ultimately lead to "transforming the world," women do not do the transforming directly.[10] There is at least one traditional Confucian who goes a step farther, arguing not just that men and women have the same natures and capacities, but also that limiting a woman's sphere of activity harms her in ways that Confucians themselves should find problematic. Luo Rufang's 16th-century contemporary Li Zhi (1527–1602 CE) is famous for many iconoclastic views. In his "A Letter in Response to the Claim that Women Cannot Learn the Way Because They Are Shortsighted," Li draws an analogy between people's capacity for learning the Way and the faculty of vision. That faculty is shared by men and women and is essentially the same. Insofar as we do find variants in people's ability to see, their sex itself has little to do with it. As evidence, Li points to numerous accounts of enlightened and capable women in history. Insofar as women of his time seem to have a more parochial understanding of the world, then, it cannot be due to their sex. The better explanation is that their experiences and education have been confined to domestic matters, to life in the inner chambers, giving them too little opportunity to see the world beyond. In other words, Li believes that history shows that women are as capable of being moral paragons as men, and furthermore that actual inequalities in enlightenment between men and women are better explained by the scope of women's and men's experiences than by sex. The clear implication of Li's letter is that the gender norms present in his society are undermining women's ability to be "farsighted"—that is, virtuous and enlightened.[11]

Several contemporary Confucian philosophers have built on claims like those of Empress Renxiaowen and Li Zhi to develop more thorough models of a feminist Confucianism. Sin-yee Chan argues that the inner-outer distinction—which the empress still clearly accepts while Li Zhi's letter challenges—actually has no deep basis in Confucianism. She shows that early Confucianism provides no basis for a difference between men's and women's moral natures and goes on to demonstrate that the subordination of women through confinement to the "inner" cannot "be justified on Confucian grounds. One can discard this Confucian conception of gender without relinquishing one's commitment to the core doctrines of early Confucianism." She concludes that patriarchal practices in China are not based in Confucian values or theory, but on "prejudices or the particular conditions of individual societies."[12] Similarly, in an earlier book I have shown that the narrow types of virtue that are traditionally envisioned as ideals for women (such as "chastity and quietude") are what feminists have called "burdened virtues." A burdened virtue is a trait that is only useful to have under conditions of oppression: it helps one to cope with one's situation, but simultaneously serves to limit one's possibilities and would not be desirable were it not for the oppressive circumstances.[13]

I noted earlier that non-hierarchical and non-fixed versions of *yin* and *yang* can ground a flexible and egalitarian way of looking at gender differences, non-binary gender, and gender fluidity. The idea is not that gender differences disappear, but rather that we reject the idea of a permanent, gender-based, hierarchical assignment of roles. Instead of limiting women to "inner" roles and men to "outer" ones—and for that matter, insisting that all people at all times must fit unambiguously into the category of "woman" or "man"—Confucianism encourages us to think about individual contributions to our relationships over time. A strong spousal relationship will be one in which each partner's distinctive (and probably changing) characteristics and goals are complemented, nourished, or perhaps subjected to healthy critique by the other's. The foundation for such mutual growth is the core Confucian virtues that I have discussed throughout this book. Often existing social "rituals" of dress and comportment will suffice for expressing one's distinctive gender profile to others, but as discussed in Chapter 17, when current rituals are too confining one must resist them and seek new ones. Finally, even within the framework of egalitarian gender relations, there will often be appropriate moments for one person to defer to another. Understanding the value of appropriate deference is key to any modern Confucianism.

19 | HIERARCHY

At age fifty-three I became a "boss," and I wasn't sure I liked it. I had spent most of my adult life up until then around college campuses and explicit hierarchies rarely seemed to intrude. Oh, I was at least somewhat aware of my privileged position as a straight, white male, and from my earliest student days I knew about some of the challenges faced by workers (my sophomore fall featured a major strike by two campus unions). But, at least in US universities, the relations among undergraduates, graduate students, and faculty members (untenured and tenured alike) are only lightly marked with hierarchical symbols or customs. For the most part, faculty act as independent contractors: there are relations of power but little overt hierarchy. I can recall struggling to answer when a school assignment led one of my daughters to wonder who my boss was. When I took over as director of my university's Center for Global Studies, for the first time I had a number of professional staff who reported to me—some of whom regularly refer to me as their "boss." I had already felt uncomfortable when I heard a previous director refer to "his staff," and now

I was apparently the "boss." What about this was rubbing me the wrong way, and what might Confucians have to say about the presence of hierarchies in our societies?

Hierarchies are rankings of people, one above another. The earliest use of the English word "hierarchy" referred to divisions of angels, but this theological meaning has little or nothing to do with modern English usage, much less with Confucian ideas. Classical Confucian texts abound in references to distinctions of "higher" and "lower"; these hierarchies are taken to mark differences in authority, ability, or degree of moral cultivation. For example, the *Analects* records Master You as stating: "It is rare for someone who has a sense of filial and fraternal responsibility to have a taste for transgressing against superiors"; a later passage adds that among the things exemplary persons detest were "those subordinates who would malign their superiors."[1] A famous passage in the *Xunzi* explains that humans are different from other creatures chiefly in our ability to form communities, which in turn come from our capacity to recognize and embrace social divisions. A related passage elaborates:

> Make clear the people's allotments, their responsibilities;
>> Assign to people proper works, arrange activities;
>> Use those having talents, grant office for abilities;
>> So none are not well ordered, nor have improprieties.[2]

Mengzi's "Five Relationships" that we met back in Chapter 13 are themselves hierarchies—father superior to son, ruler to subject, husband to wife, elder to younger—with the significant exception of the final relation: that between friends.

Do these Confucian hierarchical relations mean that the "superiors" can just order around the "inferiors" however they please? Not at all. Confucian hierarchy is in fact a dramatic critique of earlier Chinese notions of hierarchy. Instead of basing hierarchy in heredity—one inherits one's status by being born into it—Confucians argue that all people are equal by nature and differences of status are earned. Admittedly, there are some important issues with the way this thought is developed. But it is crucial to the current viability of any sort of Confucian hierarchy that from the beginning it has been based on relationships that can change. Take the relationship between ruler and subject, for example. Early Confucians emphasize the two-way responsibilities inherent in such a relationship: rulers must care for their subjects and subjects must be devoted to their rulers. Two modern scholars have suggested that a good way to capture this feature of Confucian hierarchy is to use "benefactors" and "beneficiaries" instead of "superiors" and "inferiors" to name the two sides of any given hierarchy.[3] At least in principle, the idea that hierarchy must be merited (by fulfilling one's responsibilities) means that one can fail to merit the position of "benefactor" and thus lose such a status. One of the best-known passages in *Mengzi* explains that when an ancient tyrant was killed, this was not a case of "regicide": the ruler's awful treatment of his people meant that he did not count as a "king," and so his death was the execution of a common criminal.[4]

The authority of a superior (or benefactor) thus comes from merit: what a person does or the kind of person her or she is. Sorhoon Tan calls this "authoritative" rather than "authoritarian"; an authoritarian relationship, in contrast, is based on coercion rather than excellence.[5] However, Tan and other modern scholars also acknowledge that in historical practice, authoritative ideals often slid into an authoritarian reality. In the political sphere, there were few institutionalized protections for those who would speak up against a tyrannical monarch, and despite the early rejection of a hereditary hierarchy, in practice hereditary monarchy and violent rebellion were pretty much the only games in town.[6] Another area in which reality fell far short of the ideal was in social mobility. By around 1000 CE China had developed an extensive system of civil service exams, which in principle allowed boys and young men of any social background access to positions in the sprawling government bureaucracy. Because such government positions were crucial to a family's success, the system theoretically allowed people to move up (and down) the social, professional, and political hierarchies based on their educational achievements; a famous poem maintains that "one can be a farmhand in the morning, but come to the emperor's court in the evening."[7] It is indeed important that Confucian theory emphasizes mobility, but it is also crucial that Chinese practice generally failed to deliver much movement, as many scholars have shown.

I have been emphasizing socio-political relationships, but even teacher–student relations could devolve into authoritarianism, though here student "exit" was more of a possibility. Family relationships were another difficult area. We saw earlier on that filial piety is based in part in one's response to loving concern from one's parents. Of course, parents are not always wonderful, and "mobility" or "exit" are difficult or even impossible in family contexts. Part of the answer to this is loving remonstrance (gently nudging one's parent to be better). Another dimension of

Confucians' response, though, is to call attention to other, more egalitarian relationships that are also important to us. What I have in mind here is the fifth of the Five Relationships, that between friend and friend. We exist in networks of different types of relationships, some of which will be more important than others at different points in our lives. Among other functions, friendships can provide a space without rigid hierarchical demands. In keeping with their focus on ethical improvement, Confucians believe that at least in the best kinds of friendships, we strive to aid and encourage one another. Nonetheless, relationships among friends are distinctly non-hierarchical, or at least extremely flexible. My friend is better than me at some things, and I'm his or her better in others, so we sometimes defer to and take pleasure in learning from the other. While friendship plays some role for almost all Confucian theorists, only a few elevate it above other relationships.[8]

In the face of both abstract and in-practice concerns about hierarchy, it is tempting to say that we should abandon hierarchy—and if that also means to abandon Confucianism, then so it goes. However, there are three reasons to resist such a dramatic step. First, hierarchies are extremely common in the ways we humans organize ourselves the world over, in contexts ranging from family to society to business to politics. Abandoning hierarchy might be practically or even theoretically impossible. Perhaps Xunzi is right that community depends on embracing social divisions? Second, although some forms of hierarchy seem clearly to be problematic, the Confucians may be able to help us see that other forms are healthy and even essential to desirable forms of personal growth (even aside from their role in supporting communities). If we can learn to distinguish healthy from unhealthy and determine how the former can be encouraged and the latter avoided in practice, then hierarchy starts to sound more attractive. Finally, we should keep in mind that modernity in many societies has been characterized by what Aaron Stalnaker has called a "systematic pathologization of dependence." Many commentators have begun to recognize that we are not purely autonomous creatures but in fact are always to one degree or another dependent on others. For this reason, the rejection of tradition and status in favor of free-floating, contractual relations among (putative) equals that began in Europe with the Protestant Reformation and deepened in the Enlightenment, has gone too far.[9] I wonder, in fact, if my own discomfort with being a "boss" is part of this cultural legacy. Traditional Confucianism may need some updating, but so too may our modern attitudes toward hierarchy.

* * *

There are three keys to a modern Confucian view of hierarchy. First, there are some areas where traditional views simply need to be criticized and changed. Second, in some cases we need to carve out space for new kinds of equal, non-hierarchical relations; chief among these are equality before the law and the political equality of citizens. Finally, for the remaining large number of potentially hierarchical relations, we need to clarify how a proper understanding of hierarchy (and the structures and values that support it) make it healthy. To a great extent, these healthy hierarchies are just what a traditional Confucian would expect, but as we work through the three keys in more detail, their resonance with our own, modern lives will be clear.

Let's first look at the areas in which traditional views should be changed. Insofar as our critiques are based on Confucian values, then even significant changes can still be seen as part of the ongoing renovation of a living tradition. As you'll remember this is the case for Confucianism and gender, and there needs to be a related updating of the way Confucians should understand spousal relationships.[10] The other major area where change is needed is in political relationships; "ruler–subject" should simply be abandoned and replaced with a new model of citizenship.

The second key to a modern Confucian view of hierarchy is to see that there are new sorts of relations, not recognized in traditional Confucianism, that need to be defined and defended as equal (that is, as non-hierarchical). The two most important examples are equality as subjects of the law (legal equality) and equality as citizens (political equality). Neither of these existed in traditional East Asia. Law was understood as the standing orders of the monarch, who could change the law as he desired; it also treated subjects very differently depending on social status.[11] And there was no such thing as a "citizen": the main political relationship was that between a ruler and his (or, very occasionally, her) subjects. The questions of how and why modern Confucians should embrace equality-before-the-law and a politics defined by equal citizenship are huge and complicated. Interested readers can explore these arguments elsewhere; here, I will rely on the conclusions concerning modern Confucian law and politics that I find most convincing. More important for our purposes is this question: What does this all mean for how we can live as modern Confucians? A modern Confucian citizen will be politically equal to all other citizens, which means sharing the same political rights and responsibilities. But it is worth keeping in mind that this does not mean that all political relationships are equal in every respect. In a representative democracy, in some ways we expect our representatives to defer to their constituents (as "public servants"). At the same time, we expect them not simply to do whatever the latest poll says, but to exercise judgment and act as leaders. We should be willing to defer to them at least in the sense of being willing to listen to their reasons and to accept their judgment in typical cases. It is also true that equality before the law need not erase all forms of differentiation; for example, US law does not require spouses to testify against one another, in part because to do so would undermine the bond between them. Confucian jurists will look for similar ways in which laws can enhance important relationships, but always on the basis of the idea that all individuals are subject to the same set of laws.[12]

The first two keys to modern Confucian hierarchy are both anti-hierarchical: there are important ways in which Confucians today should resist hierarchy. Lest you think that the idea of "modern Confucian hierarchy" is a joke, let me assure you that there's quite a lot of room for hierarchy left! The third key, then, is to see how hierarchy can be healthy and even crucial. As we have seen throughout this book, the related ideas of learning, growth, and improvement are central to Confucianism. A stagnant society in which no one recognizes the need to change and grow is the opposite of the Confucian ideal. In most circumstances, it is impossible to learn from others unless one at least temporarily defers to them. Stop, listen, and be open to the prospect that someone else knows more, has more experience, or is more skilled than you. You can become better (or more knowledgeable or wiser) by modelling yourself—at least in some respect—on the other. In an insightful recent essay, the contemporary Confucian scholar Joseph Chan has linked healthy hierarchies to what he calls "society as a community of learners," which recalls Kongzi's statement recorded in *Analects* 7:22, "When I am walking in a group of three people, there will surely be a teacher for me among them. I pick out the good parts and follow them; the bad parts, and change them."[13]

Sometimes such deference comes in one-off, unplanned situations. A guide, teacher, or other kind of leader may emerge from a group without bearing any prior marker of higher status in the relevant dimension. Unlike when we're following an official tour guide (who may be carrying a flag), sometimes we follow someone who stands out in an emergency situation, someone who simply "seems to know what they're doing." In many cases, though, deference emerges in predictable ways within on-going relationships. This is crucial for Confucians, because healthy hierarchy can never simply be a ranking, a bald assertion that some people have higher status than others. Instead, it must be based on an enduring pattern of interaction. On-going relationships enable positive outcomes like learning; they allow the relationships to be reciprocal, whereby both higher and lower status individuals can gain from their connection; and they make possible changes to the relationship, depending on how the parties fulfil their responsibilities. Consider a teacher–student relationship, for example. Obviously, learning is central to such a relationship, though to non-teachers it may be less obvious that teachers often learn as much from their students as the other way around. Also, it is possible for students to grow beyond their teachers; indeed, this is a mark of the teacher's success! "Teacher" is also a designation that at least in principle is maintained through continuing to merit it. Evaluations of one's teaching by students, peers, and administrators all have the possibility of leading to loss of status. Such processes are often vexed and imperfect in the real world, but the principle is a good one, especially if it helps to stimulate more learning (for example, continuing teacher education).

Learning is central to healthy hierarchy, but it is not the only justification. Hierarchies are also valuable for the ways in which they help us coordinate our behavior and express respect. Depending on the specific relationship, the ways these three factors interact will differ. Contrast the relationship between a boss and a brand-new, very junior employee, on the one hand, and that same relationship a year or two later. Early on, the coordinating function will be quite rigid and one-directional: the employee has so much to learn that he or she pretty much must be told what to do. Showing respect for the boss is appropriate but is unlikely to be that deeply felt, since the relationship is so new and shallow. Eventually, both the learning and especially the coordination should become less one-sided, as the employee's perspectives have grown, and in healthy situations respect will have grown deeper (and also in both directions).

Healthy Confucian hierarchies are sustained by several values, most of which should be familiar by this point in the book. Care for others, concerned attention to the specifics of the situations one encounters, and flexible, imaginative openness to different perspectives are all important Confucian ideas that we have already met. Armed with these values we can hope to be constructive participants in hierarchies and to resist the many ways in which potentially positive hierarchies can become unhealthy (remembering, of course, that the first key to modern Confucian hierarchy has been to critique and eliminate some traditional forms of hierarchy).

Aside from our relationships with our parents, the explicit hierarchies that modern-day people encounter most often are probably based in our workplaces. Writing this chapter has given me an opportunity to reflect on and revise my own views of being a "boss." Part of my problem, I suspect, stems from connotations of the word itself. I still don't think that we should take pleasure in "bossing others around" or "being bossy." But I can see more clearly now that organizations flourish only when they have bosses—otherwise known as leaders—who take their role seriously. Good leaders in any context earn their higher status and the whole group benefits from healthy, flexible hierarchies.

20 | CONFUCIANISM AROUND THE WORLD

The great historian Yu Ying-shih coined a powerful metaphor to describe the status of Confucianism in the modern world: in the 20th century Confucianism had become a "wandering soul." He meant that while the values and insights of Confucianism were not dead, as they were preserved by individuals both in East Asia and further afield, the institutional and cultural "embodiment" of Confucianism was gone. The imperial monarchy, classics-based educational system, and massive bureaucracy staffed by Confucians: all had disappeared over the course of a couple decades around the turn of the 20th century. The elaborate system of familial rituals was hanging on to some degree, but the twin challenges of urban modernity and communist revolution meant that Confucianism was a pale imitation of its former self.

To thrive and be relevant in the 21st century, Confucianism needs both soul and body. As I will explain further in a moment, Confucianism has from the beginning aspired to speak to all people, but—like any tradition, really—it has done so in linguistically and culturally specific ways. Therefore, it will be important to ask what the prospects are for Confucianism's renewed embodiment. To understand this, we'll look at a few important questions. What would a revived Confucianism look like in East Asia (and is this already appearing)? Might Confucianism develop outside of East Asia; for example, in the ways that Buddhism has in the United States? Finally, what about the possibilities for Confucianism joining with or piggy-backing on other traditions: Are multiple identities or piecemeal borrowing compatible with the kind of "commitment" that Confucianism requires? While it's important to consider these issues carefully, the main thing to keep in mind is that, all things considered, there are multiple paths to a bright future for the Confucian way of life.

* * *

Many statements within the founding texts of the Confucian tradition suggest that its teachings are relevant to all. For instance, Mengzi says, "All people can become a Yao or a Shun," meaning that any person anywhere has the capacity to become a sage (just like Yao or Shun).[1] The *Analects* records Kongzi saying that he wants to dwell among the Yi people outside the Chinese heartland, which leads someone to ask him: "But they are uncouth; how will you manage?" Kongzi responds, "If an exemplary person were to dwell among them, what uncouthness would there be?"[2] The implication seems to be that Confucian virtue is not limited by borders or culture but applies and can spread wherever exemplary people may go.

I think it is unquestionable that Confucian teachings have a kind of universal aspiration, potentially applicable to anyone. A bit more thought about the *Analects* passage I just quoted, though, re-introduces culture into the equation. After all, for early Confucians the question is not of relations between two equivalent cultures, but of the uncultured becoming cultured and susceptible to the exemplary person's moral influence. Part of what Kongzi envisions bringing with him to the Yi is precisely the rituals and other cultural heritage of the Zhou dynasty. As they learn to be cultured—in a quite specific way—they will cease to be uncouth even as they grow morally. Translating this into our modern context, does this mean that for Confucianism to again have a "body," a rebirth of ancient Zhou culture is required? If so, any modern Confucianism is doomed. However, Confucians for many centuries have explicitly argued that the rituals and institutions of Confucian practice can and must change with the times. The "body," that is, can be very different so long as it continues to manifest the ideas and values of the "soul." The reason that a body is necessary is that it makes possible the sharing with one another of the soul. Humaneness, harmony, a commitment to mutual moral growth, and so on: the central themes of Confucianism are accessible to all but, practically speaking, depend on relationships with actual others. So teaching, learning, and acting in Confucian ways all require a culture that is sufficiently shared and sufficiently Confucian.

What would a contemporary culture that is sufficiently shared and sufficiently Confucian look like? Let's first try to answer this question for societies in the East Asian heartland of Confucianism like South Korea, Mainland China, Japan, or Taiwan. The key thing to recognize is how infertile the soil is for the regrowth of Confucianism in these societies, for three reasons. First, each country is now governed by a modern political ideology (liberal democracy or socialist authoritarianism) that has little direct connection to traditional Confucian institutions. Second, over the last century, the dominant attitude across the region has been to criticize traditional values as inconsistent with modernity. Third, each of these societies is now much more diverse—and increasingly conscious of this diversity—than was the case one hundred or more years ago. In the view of Zhang Xianglong of Zhongshan University, the prospects for Confucian culture in China are so dire that he has argued for the establishment of "Confucian Culture Preservation Areas," nationally protected areas where self-identified Confucians could follow their culture rather like the Amish do in various parts of the United States.[3]

The main reason that Professor Zhang is so pessimistic as to think that Confucianism can only thrive in protected enclaves is that he mostly adopts a very conservative, traditionalist understanding of Confucian values and culture. (In a surprising exception to this generalization, in one of his essays Zhang argues that we can see the universal appeal of Confucianism's ideal of filial piety by looking at the relations between children and parents in the *Harry Potter* series.[4]) I think we can agree with Zhang that if to live a Confucian life, one must insist on traditional gender roles then it has little hope of flourishing in the broader world, nor should it. The argument of my chapter on gender, though, has been that a properly progressive Confucianism not only need not, but in fact should not accept traditional gender roles. Many of the intellectuals in East Asia who have been leading the way toward a distinctively modern, progressive understanding of Confucianism have underscored this point.

The other main challenge to a healthy new Confucian "body" in East Asia is politics. Scholars continue to debate the relationship between democracy and Confucianism, though I myself am sanguine about their partnership. In recent years the Chinese Communist Party (CCP) has reversed decades of criticism of Confucianism—which the CCP had long seen as an obstacle to egalitarian, socialist revolution—and begun to endorse it as part of a narrative of the revival of the Chinese nation, led by the CCP. The CCP has so thoroughly embraced markets and abandoned communism that it needs new stories to justify its leading role in China, and so has opted to emphasize economic growth and cultural nationalism. This is a dangerous path for Confucianism, however, as it risks having the values of Confucianism hollowed out to become empty slogans of the ruling party. Already, in Chinese slang to be "harmonized" now means to have been picked up by state security agents. As a result, some worry that the CCP's newfound affection for Confucianism is actually the "kiss of death" for Confucianism.[5] The many differences among East Asian societies and the difficulty of predicting the future make it impossible to say for sure how Confucianism may develop in the region. Recalling the enthusiasm for progressive Confucianism of the journalist I mentioned earlier—the more she learned about what Confucianism can be, the more her skepticism receded—we can at least say that so long as Confucianism's East Asian advocates steer a progressive course and navigate the shoals of politics, Confucianism can discover a new kind of embodiment in its original homelands.

* * *

What of Confucianism outside East Asia? What would a sufficiently shared and sufficiently Confucian culture look like there? For some context, let's first look at the cases of Chinese and American Buddhism. Certainly, the Buddha's teachings were intended as universally applicable. In a whole variety of ways, though, these teachings were bound together with and expressed through the culturally distinctive languages and practices of India. When Buddhist teachers arrived in China in the early first millennium CE, they initiated a process of mutual adaptation. China and Chinese adapted to Indian and Central Asian Buddhist language, concepts, and practices, and these in turn adapted to Chinese linguistic, conceptual, and practical proclivities. The process is fascinating and took centuries to play out. In major ways, China changed: the rise of Buddhist monasteries populated by clergy who had left their families and sworn abstinence marked a dramatic shift in Chinese society. In other ways, Buddhism changed. For one thing, the decision to become a monk or nun came to be understood within Buddhist circles as a supremely filial act because one devoted one's life to saving one's family (and all other sentient beings). Early on in this process of adaptation, the very possibility of Chinese Buddhism, not to mention the legitimacy of any distinctively Chinese Buddhist doctrines, could well have been questioned. By the end, China was a major center of world Buddhism (and, ironically, Buddhism had ceased to be a significant force in India).

Turn now to the on-going story of modern American Buddhism. It may come as a surprise to learn that, according to the latest Pew Research Center "Religious Landscape Survey," Buddhism is the fourth-largest religion in America at 0.7 percent of the population, behind Christianity (70.6 percent), Judaism (1.9 percent), and Islam (0.9 percent).[6] Scholars generally agree that there are three distinct sources of American Buddhism: "import" (Americans who have discovered Buddhism through reading or travel, thus creating a demand for Buddhism), "export" (proselytizing by Asian Buddhist organizations), and "ethnic" (when Buddhism is brought to America by Asian immigrants).[7] Thomas Tweed suggests that in the American cultural context, Buddhism has become more "Protestant" (borrowing words like "worship" and "churches"), democratic, pragmatic, and ecumenical.[8] In any event, it seems plausible to say that the Buddhist tradition is taking root in America as Americans discover its ability to speak to (and simultaneously to shape) their concerns and worldviews. In other words, culturally distinctive traditions can appeal across cultures (via potentially universal values), which thereby motivates two-way adaptation into these new contexts.

Can what has worked for Buddhism do the same for Confucianism? Some of the same challenges facing Confucianism in East Asia are also barriers to its growth in societies like the United States. For example, the lack of formal Confucian institutions (Confucianism's absent "body") makes it difficult for the "export" dynamic to play out. Chinese government-sponsored "Confucius Institutes" might play some role, even though they are mainly focused on language-teaching; but they have become embroiled in controversies surrounding their efforts to promote the political views of the People's Republic. The "ethnic" framework is also less straightforward in the case of Confucianism. To the extent that East Asian American families in America emphasize the importance of filial devotion or education, does this mean that they are Confucians? Probably yes, at least to some degree, but rarely do members of these families read Confucian texts, discuss Confucian ideas with others, or look for ways in which traditional Confucian values should develop in new ways in the new contexts of modern America. The lack of a robust, progressive institutional presence for Confucianism is once again a problem.

There are some fascinating signs of change, however, which also speak to the possibility of "import" Confucianism. Academic study of Confucianism has grown significantly over the last several decades, led by a diverse range of scholars—some with East Asian heritage, some not. For some of these scholars, their interest in Confucianism is primarily academic and historical; others are also advocates and practitioners, like long-time Harvard professor Tu Wei-ming and Boston University-based philosopher-theologian Robert Neville. Several years ago, Neville's student Bin Song was instrumental in establishing an active Facebook group dedicated to Confucianism called "Friends From Afar" (an allusion to the first chapter of the *Analects*); members discuss how to apply Confucianism in their lives. One of the University of Chicago's chaplains explicitly identifies as Confucian and draws on Confucianism in her work. And audiences for lectures, classes, and books on Confucianism have often been quite impressive. In the absence of formal institutions with which to identify, might these sprouts of interest in Confucianism lead to new forms of Confucian life? In part this depends on whether Confucianism "commitment" requires that one only identify as a Confucian.

* * *

A friend who was a scholar of East Asian religion once explained to me that Japanese people often only find out what sect of Buddhism they "belong to" when a member of their family dies: family elders let the rest know which temple to contact to perform the funeral. This is not to say that Buddhism, Shinto, and perhaps other traditional religions or practices will have had no role in such a person's life previously. Certain festivals or life events call for rituals of one kind or another, and many people still think of themselves as Buddhist in a vaguer, more "spiritual" sense. In China, it is increasingly common for people to burn incense and pray at refurbished Confucian temples when their children are taking major school exams, but to look to a Daoist or Buddhist site for other sorts of worship. All this mirrors, at least to some degree, the flexible notion of religious identity that has been mainstream in East Asia (and many other parts of the world) for millennia.

Confucianism has never demanded one's sole allegiance. It does not rest on the belief in one God or one set of doctrine, as opposed to another. If you were to look back at the various Confucian "beliefs" that I have canvassed in this book, you would find things like the following:

1. Confucians believe that all people have equal moral potential.
2. Confucians believe that a fundamentally positive orientation to life is manifested, to at least some degree, in everyone.
3. Neo-Confucians believe that our natures have deep-seated orientations toward balanced interdependence and never-ending embrace of life.

4. Confucians believe that what we should become is based on what we already are. Our best selves must grow from our earlier and more basic selves.

5. Confucians believe that through study and other forms of cultivation one can gradually alter one's dispositions.

6. Confucians believe that it is possible to have a unified, harmonious, balanced self.

7. Historical Confucians believed that things were better back when the ancient sage-kings ruled than during the present day.

8. Most historical Confucians believed that the abilities, virtues, and spheres of activity of men and women were separate and unequal.

I have already argued that Confucians today should reject number 8 and need not place any weight on number 7. Numbers 3 and 6 are stronger claims than most of the rest, and some Confucians will not accept 3, at least. My main point, though, is to highlight the ease of accepting beliefs like these along with other sets of beliefs that may shape your identity. A commitment to a Confucian life is compatible with many varieties of individual or group identity.

Still, I have been emphasizing throughout this chapter the need for a sufficiently shared and sufficiently Confucian culture. Can that be found when those seeking to live as Confucians have a diverse range of other beliefs? What about piecemeal borrowing of ideas that appeal to you: Is that legitimate? Or would following only a smattering of Confucian practices constitute some kind of cultural appropriation or mere dilettantism?

One of the lessons of this book is that in important respects, life as a Confucian today will not resemble life as a Confucian centuries ago—no matter whether one is Chinese or not, no matter whether one is living in East Asia or not. Traditional cultural patterns must be "appropriated" and adapted by moderns if we are to give life to the values at the heart of the Confucian tradition. Because the idea that the external practices of Confucianism—its rituals—can change is itself deeply Confucian, there should be no problem with this form of adaptation, so long as it is built on a commitment to central Confucian goals.

Whether multiple, hyphenated identities (like Confucian-Christian or Confucian-Marxist) are sustainable depends on the details of one's non-Confucian beliefs and commitments. Christian beliefs in an afterlife are not a problem for Confucians so long as one remains resolutely focused on living a good life in this world. A Marxist belief in social justice is eminently compatible with Confucianism, but a foregrounding of struggle and revolution will be hard to square with Confucian views of harmony and non-coercion. In any of these cases, the viability of one's commitment to Confucianism will be enhanced to the extent that the vocabulary and concerns of Confucianism become better known—which once again points to the need for continuing institutional innovation to revive a Confucian "body."

What about just being inspired by one or another Confucian value without coming to identify as Confucian? Being a good global citizen entails being open to and at least somewhat interested in learning about the ways of life taught by other traditions. Allowing what you learn to act as a catalyst for your own growth is to practice what I have called rooted global philosophy.[9] It's "rooted" because it starts where you start: after all, you cannot help using your own standards as a point of departure. Maybe your values and goals are rooted in Catholicism, atheist liberalism, secular Jewish progressivism, Baptist social activism, or any number of other possibilities. The point is that from this "root," you and your framework can develop through thoughtful encounters with other traditions of thought and life. Indeed, throughout its history Confucianism has grown in just this way. Early Confucians debated with but also learned from Mohists, Daoists, and Legalists. Buddhists were the major interlocutors for Neo-Confucians, and modern "New Confucians" have had extended interactions with the ideas of Kant and Hegel. Even more recently, the conversation between Confucians and feminists is on-going. As we each seek the Way—that is, the path to the best life that we can live together with others—it only makes sense that this be an open, global conversation.

For you to take Confucianism seriously as a conversation partner, it's obviously necessary to get beyond the caricatured, "Confucius says" remarks one might find in a fortune cookie. Just cherry-picking a gnomic saying here and there cannot get at the real insights of a tradition. But neither is learning from a tradition like Confucianism as an all-or-nothing affair. Perhaps you're dissatisfied with how your education has been going and are intrigued by the Confucian approach to reading. Or the idea of life-long moral growth, a commitment to be better tomorrow than you are today, helps to give your life meaning that you'd felt lacking. Maybe like me, you've lost a loved one and value the insight that Confucians provide into how and why we mourn. These are just a few of the ways Confucianism can speak to us today. If its teachings come to shape how you think and live, how you talk and seek to share with others, then not only will you be living a better life, but you'll also be helping to give Confucianism's "wandering soul" a body once again.

FURTHER READING

There are many ways to continue your exploration of Confucianism, only some of which involve reading more. Being more caring and respectful, more nurturing and attentive, more open and engaged: these are all things that we can work on within our own lives every day. We can be more intentional about rituals, music, and reflection. Of course, reading also plays a role—especially to the extent we can read in the way that Zhu Xi recommends.

The slow, probing approach to reading that I described in Chapter 6 is most appropriate for classics, so let's begin with some recommendations for editions of Confucian texts you might want to savor. The *Analects* exists in many translations aimed at various different audiences. I find myself drawn to editions that add commentary (sometimes from traditional scholars, sometimes based on modern readings) after each passage, which helps provide context and provokes reflection. Otherwise, the *Analects* can be a very spare and even cryptic text! Here are four favorites (full citations for all books mentioned here are available in the bibliography):

- *Understanding the Analects of Confucius*, translated by Peimin Ni. Ni strives to mirror ambiguities in the original in his translation, and his comments do a lovely job of opening the text up for the reflective reader.

- *The Original Analects*, translated by E. Bruce Brooks and A. Taeko Brooks. The Brookses re-order the text in an effort to show how it may have evolved historically. More than any other edition, this effectively emphasizes that the *Analects* was not written as a single monograph.
- *Analects with Selections from Traditional Commentaries*, translated by Edward Slingerland. An accessible translation with a good balance of commentaries; also available in a briefer edition as the *Essential Analects*.
- *The Analects of Confucius: A Philosophical Translation*, translated by Roger Ames and Henry Rosemont. Ames and Rosemont take special care to articulate philosophically distinctive aspects of the text in their edition.

There are fewer editions available of the other main classics, but in each case there are excellent options:

- *Mengzi with Selections from Traditional Commentaries*, translated by Bryan Van Norden. Also available in a briefer edition as the *Essential Mengzi*.
- *Mencius*, translated by D. C. Lau.
- *Xunzi: The Complete Text*, translated by Eric Hutton.

As for Neo-Confucian original texts, we again have some terrific possibilities:

- Zhu Xi. *Learning to be a Sage*, translated by Daniel Gardner. Chapters on the broad topic of "learning" from a massive edition of Zhu Xi's conversations with students.

- Zhu Xi, *Zhu Xi: Selected Writings*, translated by Philip J. Ivanhoe et al. More comprehensive than *Learning to Be a Sage*, drawing on a range of original sources.
- Wang Yangming, *Instructions for Practical Living*. Translated by Wing-tsit Chan. A complete translation of Wang's main text, unfortunately out of print.
- Wang Yangming et al, *Readings from the Lu-Wang School of Neo-Confucianism*, translated by Philip J. Ivanhoe. Contains selections of Wang's most famous works.
- Wu Yubi. *The Journal of Wu Yubi: The Path to Sagehood*. Translated by Theresa Kelleher. Although Wu was not one of the book's main heroes, I referenced him several times and his journal is a terrific window onto what it was like to commit oneself to Confucian learning.
- *The Confucian Four Books for Women*, translated by Ann A. Pang-White. This set of four texts spans more than a millennium and includes the full text of Empress Renxiaowen's *Teaching for the Inner Court* discussed in Chapter 18.

Beyond the translations of original texts, books on Confucianism divide into those that are primarily historical and those that are more thematic—and both categories are ever-growing. There are plenty examples of each referenced in the notes to this book, so the notes to a particular chapter that interests you offer some great ideas about how to explore more deeply. Beyond that, I'll suggest a few more options here in each category, drawing on books that are not featured in the notes already.

There are several brief historical overviews of Confucianism, like Daniel K. Gardner, *Confucianism: A Very Short Introduction* and Paul Goldin, *Confucianism*. More expansive looks at the tradition are found in Tony Swain, *Confucianism in China: An Introduction*, and Yao Xinzhong, *An Introduction to Confucianism*. Another book with a historical organization that should appeal to readers of this book is Philip J. Ivanhoe, *Confucian Moral Self Cultivation*, which compares the approaches of a number of different thinkers. Specifically on Neo-Confucianism, there are two recent studies: Stephen C. Angle and Justin Tiwald, *Neo-Confucianism: A Philosophical Introduction* and JeeLoo Liu, *Neo-Confucianism: Metaphysics, Mind, and Morality*.

Some of the thematic books collect essays by various different scholars and offer excellent overviews of a given topic; examples are *Mortality in Chinese Thought*, edited by Amy Olberding and Philip J. Ivanhoe; *Nature in Asian Traditions of Thought: Essays in Environmental Philosophy*, edited by J. Baird Callicott and Roger T. Ames; and *Confucian Spirituality* (two volumes), edited by Tu Wei-ming and Mary Evelyn Tucker. Among the many single-authored topical studies, these stand out for being accessible and connected to themes of this book:

- Heidi M. Giebel, *Ethical Excellence: Philosophers, Psychologists, and Real-Life Exemplars Show Us How to Achieve It*.
- Philip J. Ivanhoe, *Confucian Reflections: Ancient Wisdom for Modern Times*.
- Amy Olberding, *The Wrong of Rudeness*.
- Edward Slingerland, *Trying Not to Try: The Art and Science of Spontaneity*.
- Anna Sun, *Confucianism as a World Religion: Contested Histories and Contemporary Realities*.

- Yu Dan, *Confucius from the Heart: Ancient Wisdom for Today's World*.

Finally, let's not forget that there is a world of insights beyond those of the Confucian tradition, as the other books in Oxford's *Guides to the Good Life* series make eminently clear!

NOTES

CHAPTER 1
1. Sun, *Confucianism as a World Religion: Contested Histories and Contemporary Realities.*

CHAPTER 2
1. Strictly speaking, "Yangming" is actually a nickname that Wang adopted; his adult given name is Shouren, so he can also be called Wang Shouren. But both in Chinese and in English, it is far more common to refer to him as Wang Yangming.
2. Some scholars have begun referring to the tradition as "Ruism," based on the pronunciation of the Chinese term most commonly used to designate this tradition in Chinese (namely, *Ru*). "Confucianism" is vastly more recognizable to English readers than "Ruism," though, and I do not find the arguments put forward on behalf of "Ruism" to be persuasive. For an alternative view and some debate, see the comments in Angle, "Should We Use 'Ruism' Instead of 'Confucianism'?"
3. LY 7:1.
4. MC 1A:4.

CHAPTER 3
1. Mt 23:9.
2. LY 1:2.
3. LY 2:5.
4. LY 4:18.
5. LY 2:7.
6. LY 2:8.
7. LY 4:19.
8. MC 7A:17.
9. Munro, *A Chinese Ethics for the New Century: The Ch'ien Mu Lectures in History and Culture, and Other Essays on Science and Confucian Ethics,* 14; cited and discussed in Sarkissian, "Recent Approaches to Confucian Filial Morality," 9.
10. Ivanhoe, "Filial Piety as a Virtue," 299.

11. See Swanton's insightful discussion in Swanton, *Virtue Ethics: A Pluralistic View*, ch. 5.

12. Ivanhoe, "Filial Piety as a Virtue," 305.

13. Rosemont Jr. and Ames, *The Chinese Classic of Family Reverence: A Philosophical Translation of the Xiaojing*, 1.

14. Greene, "30 Years Ago, Romania Deprived Thousands of Babies of Human Contact."

15. XZ 29/4. Citations to *Xunzi* list the chapter number followed by the line number in Xunzi, *Xunzi: The Complete Text*.

16. LY 13:18.

17. MC 5A:2.

18. Ivanhoe, "Filial Piety as a Virtue," 310.

19. See Giebel, *Ethical Excellence: Philosophers, Psychologists, and Real-Life Exemplars Show Us How to Achieve It*, ch.14, for a marvelous reflection on filial piety with difficult parents.

CHAPTER 4

1. Olberding, *The Wrong of Rudeness: Learning Modern Civility From Ancient Chinese Philosophy*.

2. Tan, *Confucian Democracy: A Deweyan Reconstruction*, 84.

3. Olberding, *The Wrong of Rudeness: Learning Modern Civility From Ancient Chinese Philosophy*, ch. 7.

4. MC 4A:17.

5. This example builds on Bryan Van Norden's suggestion in Mengzi, *Mengzi: With Selections From Traditional Commentaries*, 97.

6. Depending on various details, these actions may also violate the laws against sexual harassment or assault, but for our present purposes the law is irrelevant. For more on Confucians' views of law, see Angle, *Contemporary Confucian Political Philosophy: Toward Progressive Confucianism*.

7. See LY 2:23 and LY 9:1.

8. Zhu, 《朱子全書》 [*Complete Works of Master Zhu*], vol. 22, 1796.

9. For examples of more conservative views, see my discussion in Angle, *Contemporary Confucian Political Philosophy: Toward Progressive Confucianism*, ch. 6. Contemporary Confucians who argue explicitly for the need to critique existing rituals include Huang, *Voice from the East: The Chinese Theory of Justice* and Neville, *The Good is One, Its Manifestations Many: Confucian Essays on Metaphysics, Morals, Rituals, Institutions, and Genders*, esp. ch. 15.

10. Olberding, *The Wrong of Rudeness: Learning Modern Civility from Ancient Chinese Philosophy*, 112.

11. Olberding, *The Wrong of Rudeness: Learning Modern Civility from Ancient Chinese Philosophy*, 113. In some parts of today's world, such behavior may in fact put one in danger of arrest and execution.

12. Admittedly, what one communicates by holding a door is not entirely up to one's own intentions. In a social context in which many still take door-holding as a symbol of patriarchy, some might read one's behavior as patriarchal. In brief, one-off encounters this is difficult to mitigate; over time and coupled with other sorts of more obviously anti-patriarchal behavior, it must be hoped that your intention will become clearer.

CHAPTER 5

1. De Waal, *Mama's Last Hug: Animal Emotions and What They Tell Us About Ourselves*.

2. MC 2A:6.

3. A famous debate among Korean Neo-Confucians concerned precisely this question; see Kalton, *The Four-Seven Debate: An Annotated Translation of the Most Famous Controversy in Korean Neo-Confucian Thought*.

4. XZ 23/2f.

5. MC 6A:8.

6. MC 6A:15.

7. Angle and Tiwald, *Neo-Confucianism: A Philosophical Introduction*, 28–29; "impure" versus "imbalanced" represent different theoretical developments of the core idea of vital stuff.

8. Flanagan, *The Geography of Morals: Varieties of Moral Possibility*, 56.

9. Flanagan, *The Geography of Morals: Varieties of Moral Possibility*, 72.

10. Flanagan, *The Geography of Morals: Varieties of Moral Possibility*, 106–107.

11. MC 2A:6.

12. MC 1B:10.

13. Chan, "Democratic Equality or Confucian Hierarchy?", as discussed further in Chapter 17.

14. Wu, *The Journal of Wu Yubi: The Path to Sagehood*, 41 and 31.

CHAPTER 6

1. Zhu, *Learning to be a Sage*, 143.

2. LY 3:8; see Goldin, "Reception of the *Odes* in the Warring States Era," 31.

3. Zhu, *Learning to be a Sage*, 132. See also XZ 1/129 on reciting the classics.

4. Wu, *The Journal of Wu Yubi: The Path to Sagehood*, 18.

5. Wu, *The Journal of Wu Yubi: The Path to Sagehood*, 30.

6. MC 5A:4.

7. For more on the idea of "commitment," see Chapter 11.

8. LY 8:8.

9. Zhu, *Learning to be a Sage*, 128, modified.

10. Martha Nussbaum, *Love's Knowledge: Essays on Philosophy and Literature*.

11. MC 7B:3.

12. XZ 1/71-2.

13. Stalnaker, *Mastery, Dependence, and the Ethics of Authority*, 165.

14. Quoted in Tucker, "Skepticism and the Neo-Confucian Canon: Itō Jinsai's Philosophical Critique of the *Great Learning*," 13; see also my related discussion in Angle, *Sagehood: The Contemporary Significance of Neo-Confucian Philosophy*, 148.

15. Quoted in Tucker, "Skepticism and the Neo-Confucian Canon: Itō Jinsai's Philosophical Critique of the *Great Learning*," 13.

16. For example, the 17th-century Confucian Huang Zongxi (1610–1695) proposed that books not conducive to Confucian governance should be burned; see Huang, *Waiting for the Dawn*, 107, and discussion in Chan, "Huang Zongxi as a Republican: A Theory of Governance for Confucian Democracy."

17. Zhu, *Learning to be a Sage*, 153.

18. Zhu, *Learning to be a Sage*, 152–153.

19. Goldin, "Reception of the *Odes* in the Warring States Era," 31.

20. Roth, *Safe Enough Spaces: A Pragmatist's Approach to Inclusion, Free Speech, and Political Correctness on College Campuses*.

21. Nussbaum, "Undemocratic Vistas."

CHAPTER 7

1. Murray, *Crosstown Traffic: Jimi Hendrix and the Post-War Rock 'n' Roll Revolution*, 24.

2. Murray, *Crosstown Traffic: Jimi Hendrix and the Post-War Rock 'n' Roll Revolution*, 195.

3. Clague, "'This is America': Jimi Hendrix's Star Spangled Banner Journey as Psychedelic Citizenship," 455.

4. Clague, "'This is America': Jimi Hendrix's Star Spangled Banner Journey as Psychedelic Citizenship," 459.

5. Clague, "'This is America': Jimi Hendrix's Star Spangled Banner Journey as Psychedelic Citizenship," 451.

6. See Ivanhoe, *Confucian Reflections: Ancient Wisdom for Modern Times*, ch. 4 on the "diagnostic" function of music.

7. XZ 20/61. For discussion of contemporary evidence and analysis of what Robinson has called the "jazzercise effect," see Harold, "On the Ancient Idea That Music Shapes Character," 346.

8. XZ 20/62.

9. Cook, "Musical Cultivation in the 'Xiu Wen' Chapter of the *Shuoyuan*," 391.

10. Harold, "On the Ancient Idea That Music Shapes Character," 349.

11. See Harold, "On the Ancient Idea That Music Shapes Character," 349, and the evidence he cites there.

12. For example, Tatum, "The Link Between Rap Music and Youth Crime and Violence: A Review of the Literature and Issues for Future Research" reports that studies examining the association between rap music and youth violence are "virtually nonexistent and do not consistently support a cause-effect relationship"; whereas Van Oosten, Peter, and Valkenburg, "The Influence of Sexual Music Videos on Adolescents' Misogynistic Beliefs: The Role of Video Content, Gender, and Affective Engagement" find that sexual music videos do have certain kinds of effects (principally, increasing adolescent girls' acceptance of female token resistance—i.e., the notion that women say "no" to sex when they actually mean "yes").

13. Cook, "*Yue Ji*—Record of Music: Introduction, Translation, Notes, and Commentary," 42.

14. See the further discussion of this topic in Chapter 12.

15. LY 3:25.

16. LY 15:11.

17. LY 17:28.

18. Cook, "*Yue Ji*—Record of Music: Introduction, Translation, Notes, and Commentary," 32, modified.

19. The two passages from the *Analects* use the word "*sheng*" for sound; the *Record of Music* passage uses "*yin*." In the latter text, there is a difference between *sheng* and *yin*, but this difference is not important in the present context. See Cook, "*Yue Ji*—Record of Music: Introduction, Translation, Notes, and Commentary," 19–20 for some discussion.

20. Cook, "*Yue Ji*—Record of Music: Introduction, Translation, Notes, and Commentary," 61, slightly modified.

21. MC 1B:1.

22. MC 7A:14; see discussion at Cook, "Unity and Diversity in the Musical Thought of Warring States China," 276 n67.

23. Ivanhoe, *Confucian Reflections: Ancient Wisdom for Modern Times*, 52.

24. Sartwell, "Confucius and Country Music," 252. Sartwell is drawing in part on MC 4A:27.

25. See Higgins, "Confucius' Opposition to the 'New Music '," 310 on attempts to reconstruct Zhou ritual music.

26. Bates, "A Different National Anthem, Before the Nation Was Ready for it."

27. Bates, "A Different National Anthem, Before the Nation Was Ready for it."

CHAPTER 8

1. See Israel, *Doing Good and Ridding Evil in Ming China: The Political Career of Wang Yangming*.

2. LY 1:4.
3. See LY 2:9, 4:17, and 12:4.
4. MC 4B28.
5. This is partly because of the "fundamental attribution error," whereby we are more likely to explain others' errant behavior as resulting from deep aspects of their personalities, whereas we explain our own mistakes as resulting from situational pressures outside our control.
6. Confucians well understand the ways in which our dress and body language can encourage others—often subconsciously—to respond in positive or less positive ways, which is one of the reasons for their emphasis on ritual, as we have seen in Chapter 4.
7. Wang, *Instructions for Practical Living*, 272.
8. Van Norden, *Virtue Ethics and Consequentialism in Early Chinese Philosophy*, 232. Also relevant here is Xunzi's notion of "approval" (*ke*), which similarly can involve a process of conscious cultivation. See Angle, "Is Conscientiousness a Virtue? Confucian Answers," 189–190.
9. MC 6A:15.
10. LY 15:24.
11. LY 6:30.
12. LY 2:15. See also LY 19:6 for a similar sentiment.
13. MC 7A4.
14. Justin Tiwald has written insightfully about the nuanced analyses of sympathetic understanding by Zhu Xi and others. Tiwald distinguishes between extension that depends on inference, which is closely tied to "self-focused empathy," and a direct extension which is tied to "other-focused empathy." He writes that for Zhu Xi, "self-focused empathy is—for flawed moral agents like ourselves—a necessary and useful means by which we can better understand and care for others, but ultimately it is the ladder we must kick away in favor of purely other-focused empathy." Tiwald, "Zhu Xi on Self-Focused Vs. Other-Focused Empathy," 964.
15. See Yearley, "Freud and China: The Pursuit of the Self and Other Fugitive Notions."
16. For some examples, see Slingerland, "The Situationist Critique and Early Confucian Virtue Ethics"; Sarkissian, "Minor Tweaks, Major Payoffs: The Problems and Promise of Situationism in Moral Philosophy"; and Angle, "Seeing Confucian 'Active Moral Perception' in Light of Contemporary Psychology."
17. Wu, *The Confucian's Progress: Autobiographical Writings in Traditional China*.
18. Chan, "Chu Hsi and Quiet Sitting."
19. Mabuchi, " 'Quiet Sitting' in Neo-Confucianism."
20. Bin Song, a contemporary Confucian scholar and practitioner, has been sharing insights and instructions for quiet sitting in a modern, Anglophone context; see https://binsonglive.wpcomstaging.com/.

CHAPTER 9

1. See MC 7A3 for an expression of this idea.
2. MC 2A2.
3. Chan, "Neo-Confucian Philosophical Poems," 11.
4. Woodruff, *Reverence: Renewing a Forgotten Virtue.*
5. See Angle and Tiwald, *Neo-Confucianism: A Philosophical Introduction,* 151.
6. See Angle, *Sagehood: The Contemporary Significance of Neo-Confucian Philosophy,* 154 and Angle, "Seeing Confucian 'Active Moral Perception' in Light of Contemporary Psychology."
7. Murdoch, "On 'God' and 'Good,'" 59.
8. Olberding, *The Wrong of Rudeness: Learning Modern Civility from Ancient Chinese Philosophy,* 30. See also Slingerland, *Trying Not to Try: The Art and Science of Spontaneity.*
9. Narvaez, "Moral Chronicity and Social Information Processing: Tests of a Social Cognitive Approach to the Moral Personality," 981. See also Angle, "Seeing Confucian 'Active Moral Perception' in Light of Contemporary Psychology."
10. Angle, "Seeing Confucian 'Active Moral Perception' in Light of Contemporary Psychology," 165. See also Narvaez and Lapsely, "The Psychological Foundations of Everyday Morality and Moral Expertise" and Colby and Damon, *Some Do Care: Contemporary Lives of Moral Commitment.*
11. For example, see the work of the Center for Humane Technology (https://humanet ech.com/).
12. Angle, *Sagehood: The Contemporary Significance of Neo-Confucian Philosophy,* 186.
13. Woodruff, *Reverence: Renewing a Forgotten Virtue,* 5. See also the discussion of Confucianism and humor in Bell, *China's New Confucianism: Politics and Everyday Life in a Changing Society,* ch. 9.
14. See, for example, Joshua Rothman's insightful but ultimately unconvincing essay "A New Theory of Distraction," a review of Crawford, *The World Beyond Your Head: Becoming an Individual in an Age of Distraction.*

CHAPTER 10

1. Van Norden and Tiwald, *Readings in Later Chinese Philosophy.*
2. Tan, *Confucian Democracy: A Deweyan Reconstruction,* 126.
3. Van Norden and Tiwald, *Readings in Later Chinese Philosophy.*
4. LY 2:21.
5. Delmas, "A Duty to Resist: When Disobedience Should be Uncivil," 10.
6. LY 3:1.
7. LY 9:3.
8. LY 2:3.

9. See Angle, "Human Rights and Harmony," 87–89; and Kim, "The Virtue of Incivility: Confucian Communitarianism Beyond Docility."

10. LY 8:13.

11. LY 12:11; Chan, "天下無道，我們如何安身立命？ [If the Way Does Not Prevail, Where Shall We Take Our Stand?]."

12. Hourdequin, "Engagement, Withdrawal, and Social Reform: Confucian and Contemporary Perspectives," 369.

13. LY 18:6.

CHAPTER 11

1. Wu, The Journal of Wu Yubi: The Path to Sagehood.

2. LY 2:4.

3. LY 4:9.

4. LY 4:4.

5. For more discussion and other relevant passages, see Angle, Sagehood: The Contemporary Significance of Neo-Confucian Philosophy, §7.1. It is more conventional to translate zhi as "will," but as I argue in Sagehood, "commitment" does a much better job of matching what the Chinese concept means.

6. "The Origin of New Year's Resolutions"; Waxman, "Trying to Get in Shape in 2020? Here's the History Behind the Common New Year's Resolution."

7. Crockett, "Are Gym Memberships Worth the Money?"; Roos, "January 12: The Date Most New Year's Resolutions Will Slip."

8. Statements of the Twelve Steps are readily available online; see https://www.aa.org/assets/en_US/smf-121_en.pdf.

9. Alcoholics Anonymous World Services Inc., "Frequently Asked Questions About A.A."

10. Alcoholics Anonymous World Services Inc., Alcoholics Anonymous: The Story of How Many Thousands of Men and Women Have Recovered from Alcoholism.

11. For some discussion, see https://plato.stanford.edu/entries/game-theory/#Com.

12. MC 1A:7.

13. Zhu, Learning to be a Sage, 104.

14. Zhu, Learning to be a Sage, 106.

15. Stalnaker, Mastery, Dependence, and the Ethics of Authority.

16. Hallie, Lest Innocent Blood be Shed: The Story of the Village of Le Chambon and How Goodness Happened There.

17. Justin Tiwald and I came up with this terminology in Angle and Tiwald, Neo-Confucianism: A Philosophical Introduction, 149–150.

18. Xu, 《中國人性論史》 [History of Chinese Human Nature].

19. LY 15:32.

20. MC 4B:28.

21. MC 7A:3.
22. Angle and Tiwald, *Neo-Confucianism: A Philosophical Introduction*.
23. LY 11:12.
24. For some discussion, see Huff, "Servants of Heaven: The Place of Virtue in the Confucian Cosmos" and Angle, "Tian as Cosmos in Zhu Xi's Neo-Confucianism."
25. Parks Daloz et al, *Common Fire: Leading Lives of Commitment in a Complex World*, 177.

CHAPTER 12

1. https://www.youtube.com/watch?v = Whde50AacZs.
2. LY 7A:4.
3. XZ 19/289-291; for modern scholarship and its similarity to Confucian insights, see Slingerland, "The Situationist Critique and Early Confucian Virtue Ethics." and Mower, "Situationism and Confucian Virtue Ethics."
4. LY 5:25.
5. LY 11:21.
6. See Olberding's discussion of Zigong the "technician," versus Zilu the "clown," in Olberding, " 'Ascending the Hall': Style and Moral Improvement in the *Analects*."
7. MC 7A:4.
8. Fuji, 《朱熹思想結構探索》 [*Research on the Structure of Zhu Xi's Thought*], ch. 1.
9. Seligman et al, *Ritual and Its Consequences: An Essay in the Limits of Sincerity*, 107.
10. Seligman et al, *Ritual and Its Consequences: An Essay in the Limits of Sincerity*, 128.
11. Seligman et al, *Ritual and Its Consequences: An Essay in the Limits of Sincerity*, 168.
12. Seligman et al, *Ritual and Its Consequences: An Essay in the Limits of Sincerity*, 107.
13. For a discussion that inspired these thoughts, see Nussbaum, "Perception and Revolution: *The Princess Casamaaima* and the Political Imagination."

CHAPTER 13

1. I gather it's not really a city park, but jointly owned private property.
2. https://www.poetryfoundation.org/poems/44266/mending-wall.
3. Murdoch, "The Sovereignty of the Good Over Other Concepts," 104.
4. Parker, "The Gift."
5. Parker, "The Gift."
6. MC 7B:24.
7. Wang, *Instructions for Practical Living*, 44, modified.
8. https://implicit.harvard.edu/implicit/takeatest.html.
9. Bandura, "Moral Disengagement in the Perpetration of Inhumanities," 193.
10. MC 1A:7.
11. MC 7A:4.

12. Quoted in Ivanhoe, *Oneness: East Asian Conceptions of Virtue, Happiness, and How We Are All Connected*, 47–48, slightly modified.

13. Slote, *Moral Sentimentalism*, 15.

14. See Ivanhoe, *Oneness: East Asian Conceptions of Virtue, Happiness, and How We Are All Connected* and Ivanhoe et al, *The Oneness Hypothesis: Beyond the Boundary of the Self* for more on this theme.

15. For psychology, Putilin, "Tribalism and Universalism: Reflections and Scientific Evidence" is a good example; for philosophers, Rorty, "Human Rights, Rationality, and Sentimentality" is particularly significant.

16. Wang, *Instructions for Practical Living*, 222–223, modified.

17. MC 3A:4.

18. Van Norden and Tiwald, *Readings in Later Chinese Philosophy*, 135.

19. Tu, "The Continuity of Being: Chinese Visions of Nature."

CHAPTER 14

1. https://www.transparency.org/en/cpi/2019/results/chn.

2. LY 13:18.

3. MC 5A:3.

4. Translation from Angle, *Sagehood: The Contemporary Significance of Neo-Confucian Philosophy*, 62.

5. Translation from Cook, "Unity and Diversity in the Musical Thought of Warring States China," 67.

6. Cook, "Unity and Diversity in the Musical Thought of Warring States China," 67–71.

7. LY 13:23.

8. Wang, *The Philosophical Letters of Wang Yang-Ming*, 122, modified. Ching notes that the example of an infant crying all day, and this being characterized as the "extreme of harmony" comes from *Daode Jing*, 55.

9. Wang, *Instructions for Practical Living*, 230.

10. Stohr, "Moral Cacophony: When Continence Is a Virtue," 339.

11. Stohr, "Moral Cacophony: When Continence Is a Virtue," 342–343.

12. Stohr, "Moral Cacophony: When Continence Is a Virtue," 343.

13. Stohr, "Moral Cacophony: When Continence Is a Virtue," 343.

14. Zhu and Lu, *Reflections on Things At Hand*, 188, modified.

15. MC 7A:2.

16. Ing, *The Vulnerability of Integrity in Early Confucian Thought*.

17. XZ 17.

CHAPTER 15

1. Alitto, *The Last Confucian: Liang Shu-Ming and the Chinese Dilemma of Modernity*, 3.

2. Wolf, "Moral Saints," 419.

3. Wolf, "Moral Saints," 436.

4. See generally the essays in Hadot, *Philosophy as a Way of Life: Spiritual Exercises from Socrates to Foucault.*

5. Barnes, *The Complete Works of Aristotle*, 1141b.

6. Yu, *The Ethics of Confucius and Aristotle: Mirrors of Virtue*, 204.

7. Flescher, *Heroes, Saints, & Ordinary Morality*, 219.

8. Flescher, *Heroes, Saints, & Ordinary Morality*, 183.

9. Wolf, "Moral Saints."

10. For discussion of the evolution of the term "sage," see Angle, *Sagehood: The Contemporary Significance of Neo-Confucian Philosophy*, ch 1.

11. For references, see Angle, "Is Conscientiousness a Virtue? Confucian Answers," 186–188.

12. MC 6A:7.

13. Zhu, *Further Reflections on Things At Hand*, 152, modified.

14. Stalnaker, *Overcoming Our Evil: Human Nature and Spiritual Exercises in Xunzi and Augustine*, 191.

15. Stalnaker, *Overcoming Our Evil: Human Nature and Spiritual Exercises in Xunzi and Augustine*, 252.

16. For more discussion of this theme and some examples, see Angle, *Sagehood: The Contemporary Significance of Neo-Confucian Philosophy*, 17.

17. Swanton, *Virtue Ethics: A Pluralistic View*, 204–205.

18. MC 5B:1.

19. Angle, *Sagehood: The Contemporary Significance of Neo-Confucian Philosophy*, 143–144.

20. Flanagan, *Varieties of Moral Personality: Ethics and Psychological Realism*, 29–30.

CHAPTER 16

1. LY 11:12.

2. Plato, *Complete Works*, 58 (66e).

3. Ivanhoe, "Death and Dying in the Analects," 137–138.

4. Gosetti-Ferencei, *On Being and Becoming: An Existentialist Approach to Life.*

5. Olberding and Ivanhoe, *Mortality in Chinese Thought*, chs. 1–3.

6. Ivanhoe, "Death and Dying in the Analects," 139.

7. LY 8:13.

8. LY 15:9.

9. MC 6A:10.

10. LY 16.12.

11. LY 6:10.

12. LY 11:9.

13. MC 7A:2.

14. Ivanhoe, "Death and Dying in the Analects," 140. Note that in LY 11:10 Kongzi responds to his students' criticism for having lost control of his emotions by

saying, "Have I lost control of myself? If not for this man, for whom then should I lose control?"

15. LY 19:14.

16. Olberding, "I Know Not "Seems": Grief for Parents in the *Analects*," 161.

17. Olberding, "I Know Not "Seems": Grief for Parents in the *Analects*," 168.

18. Olberding, "Slowing Death Down: Mourning in the Analects," 144.

19. Tavor, "Embodying the Dead: Ritual as Preventative Therapy in Chinese Ancestor Worship and Funerary Practices," 35.

20. Tavor, "Embodying the Dead: Ritual as Preventative Therapy in Chinese Ancestor Worship and Funerary Practices," 40.

21. Yang, "对于儒教之为教的社会学思考 [Sociological Reflections on the Religiosity of Confucianism]," 3; see also discussion in Billioud, "The Revival of Confucianism in the Sphere of Mores and the Reactivation of the Civil Religion Debate in China."

22. Yang, "Confucianism as Cvil Religion."

23. Zhu, *Further Reflections on Things At Hand*, #13.30.

24. Peng, "Death as the Ultimate Concern in Neo-Confucian Tradition: Wang Yangming's Followers as an Example."

25. Olberding, "Other People Die and *That* is the Problem."

CHAPTER 17

1. Angle, 《当代儒家政治哲学：进步儒学发凡》 [*Contemporary Confucian Political Philosophy: Toward Progressive Confucianism*].

2. MacIntyre, *Whose Justice? Which Rationality?*, 326. See also Shils, *Tradition*; MacIntyre, *Three Rival Versions of Moral Enquiry: Encyclopedia, Genealogy, and Tradition: Being Gifford Lectures Delivered in the University of Edinburgh in 1988*; Nussbaum and Sen, "Internal Criticism and the Indian Rationalist Tradition."

3. Feng, 《三松堂全集》 [*Collected Works of Feng Youlan*], 4.

4. Angle, "Review of *a Confucian Constitutional Order: How China's Ancient Past Can Shape Its Political Future* By Jiang Qing."

5. Weber, "Science as a Vocation."

6. If you would like to explore more deeply what Zhu Xi and his brethren meant by ideas like Pattern, see Angle and Tiwald, *Neo-Confucianism: A Philosophical Introduction*.

7. Jiang, *A Confucian Constitutional Order: How China's Ancient Past Can Shape Its Political Future*.

8. For an introduction, see Angle, *Contemporary Confucian Political Philosophy: Toward Progressive Confucianism*.

9. Munro, *The Concept of Man in Ancient China*.

10. MC 4B:32 and 6B:2.

11. Chan, *From Sage-Kings to Confucian Republic: The Political Theories of 'Jiaohua'*.
12. Angle, "Replacing Liberal Confucianism With Progressive Confucianism."
13. Quoted in Tang, 《德性与政治：牟宗三新儒家政治哲学研究》 [*Virtue and Politics: Research on Mou Zongsan's New Confucian Political Philosophy*].

CHAPTER 18

1. Jiang, "Only Confucians Can Make a Place for Modern Women."
2. See Raphals, *Sharing the Light: Representations of Women and Virtue in Early China*, 142 and Rosenlee, *Confucianism and Women: A Philosophical Interpretation*, 66.
3. Interestingly, Chinese medical texts do treat *yin* and *yang* in very much this way, as existing in different and changing balances within both men and women. See Raphals, *Sharing the Light: Representations of Women and Virtue in Early China*, 142 and ch. 7.
4. Chan, "Would Confucianism Allow Two Men to Share a Peach? Compatibility Between Ancient Confucianism and Homosexuality."
5. Rosenlee, *Confucianism and Women: A Philosophical Interpretation*, 84–85.
6. From the female scholar and author Ban Zhao's *Lessons for Women*, composed around 100 CE; translation from Pang-White, *The Confucian Four Books for Women: A New Translation of the Nü Sishu and the Commentary of Wang Xiang*, 54.
7. Of course, I do not mean to deny that these traditions can—and perhaps should be—feminist; for example, see Gross, *Buddhism After Patriarchy: A Feminist History, Analysis, and Reconstruction of Buddhism*.
8. For more details and references, see Angle and Tiwald, *Neo-Confucianism: A Philosophical Introduction*, 174–175.
9. Pang-White, *The Confucian Four Books for Women: A New Translation of the Nü Sishu and the Commentary of Wang Xiang*, 176.
10. Pang-White, *The Confucian Four Books for Women: A New Translation of the Nü Sishu and the Commentary of Wang Xiang*, 168 and 142.
11. See Angle and Tiwald, *Neo-Confucianism: A Philosophical Introduction*, 177–178 and Lee, "Li Zhi and John Stuart Mill: A Confucian Feminist Critique of Liberal Feminism."
12. Chan, "Gender Relationship Roles in the *Analects* and the *Mencius*," 115 and 128.
13. Angle, *Contemporary Confucian Political Philosophy: Toward Progressive Confucianism*, ch. 7. See also Lisa Tessman, *Burdened Virtues: Virtue Ethics for Liberatory Struggles*.

CHAPTER 19

1. LY 1:2 and LY 17:24.
2. XZ 9/322 and XZ 12/283.

3. Rosemont Jr. and Ames, *The Chinese Classic of Family Reverence: a Philosophical Translation of the Xiaojing*, 49–50.

4. MC 1B:8.

5. Tan, "Authoritative Master Kong (Confucius) in an Authoritarian Age."

6. Allan, *Buried Ideas: Legends of Abdication and Ideal Government in Early Chinese Bamboo-Slip Manuscripts*.

7. Quoted in Bai, *Against Political Equality: The Confucian Case*, 86.

8. Dimberg, *The Sage and Society: The Life and Thought of Ho Hsin-Yin*.

9. Stalnaker, *Mastery, Dependence, and the Ethics of Authority*, 24.

10. For an article-length discussion of why modern Confucians must recast spousal relationships along egalitarian lines, see Angle, "Confucianism on Human Relations: Progressive or Conservative?"

11. Stephens, *Order and Discipline in China: The Shanghai Mixed Court 1911–27*.

12. Angle, *Sagehood: The Contemporary Significance of Neo-Confucian Philosophy*, 217–218.

13. Chan, "Democratic Equality or Confucian Hierarchy?"

CHAPTER 20

1. MC 6B:2.

2. LY 9:13.

3. Zhang, "成立儒家文化特区或保护区的理由与方式 [Reasons and Methods for Creating Confucian Special Cultural Zones or Protection Zones]."

4. Zhang, 《家与孝：从中西间视野看》 [Family and Filial Piety: As Viewed From Between China and the West], ch. 8.

5. Peng, "儒学复兴的深思 [Reflections on the Revival of Confucianism]."

6. https://www.pewforum.org/religious-landscape-study/.

7. Prebish, *Buddhism—The American Experience*.

8. Quoted in Prebish, *Buddhism—The American Experience*.

9. Angle, *Sagehood: The Contemporary Significance of Neo-Confucian Philosophy*.

BIBLIOGRAPHY

Alcoholics Anonymous World Services Inc. "Frequently Asked Questions About A.A." https://www.aa.org/assets/en_US/p-2_faqAboutAA.pdf.

Alcoholics Anonymous World Services Inc. *Alcoholics Anonymous: The Story of How Many Thousands of Men and Women Have Recovered from Alcoholism.* New York: Alcoholics Anonymous World Services Inc., 2001.

Alitto, Guy S. *The Last Confucian: Liang Shu-Ming and the Chinese Dilemma of Modernity.* Berkeley: University of California Press, 1979.

Allan, Sarah. *Buried Ideas: Legends of Abdication and Ideal Government in Early Chinese Bamboo-Slip Manuscripts.* Albany: SUNY Press, 2015.

Angle, Stephen C. "Human Rights and Harmony." *Human Rights Quarterly* 30 (2008): 76–94.

Angle, Stephen C. *Sagehood: The Contemporary Significance of Neo-Confucian Philosophy.* New York: Oxford University Press, 2009.

Angle, Stephen C. *Contemporary Confucian Political Philosophy: Toward Progressive Confucianism.* Cambridge, UK: Polity Press, 2012.

Angle, Stephen C. "Is Conscientiousness a Virtue? Confucian Answers." In *Virtue Ethics and Confucianism,* edited by Stephen C. Angle and Michael Slote, 182–191. New York: Routledge, 2013.

Angle, Stephen C. "Review of a *Confucian Constitutional Order: How China's Ancient Past Can Shape Its Political Future* By Jiang Qing." *Philosophy East & West* 64, no. 2 (2014): 502–506.

Angle, Stephen C. "Seeing Confucian 'Active Moral Perception' in Light of Contemporary Psychology." In *The Philosophy and Psychology of Virtue: An Empirical Approach to Character and Happiness,* edited by Nancy Snow and Franco Trivigno, 163–180. New York: Routledge, 2014.

Angle, Stephen C. 安靖如. 《当代儒家政治哲学：进步儒学发凡》[*Contemporary Confucian Political Philosophy: Toward Progressive Confucianism*]. Translated by Hua Han. Nanchang: Jiangxi People's Press, 2015.

Angle, Stephen C. "Should We Use 'Ruism' Instead of 'Confucianism'?" http://warpweftandway.com/should-instead-confucianism/, 2016.

Angle, Stephen C. "Tian as Cosmos in Zhu Xi's Neo-Confucianism." *Dao: A Journal of Comparative Philosophy* 17 (2018): 169–185.

Angle, Stephen C. "Replacing Liberal Confucianism with Progressive Confucianism." *Journal of Confucian Philosophy and Culture* 32 (2019): 43–65.

Angle, Stephen C. "Confucianism on Human Relations: Progressive or Conservative?" In *Human Beings or Human Becomings: A Conversation With Confuciaism on the Concept of the Person*, edited by Peter D. Hershock and Roger T. Ames, 187–214. Albany: SUNY Press, 2021.

Angle, Stephen C., and Justin Tiwald. *Neo-Confucianism: A Philosophical Introduction*. Oxford: Polity Press, 2017.

Aristotle. *The Complete Works of Aristotle*. Edited by Jonathan Barnes. Princeton: Princeton University Press, 1984.

Bai, Tongdong. *Against Political Equality: The Confucian Case*. Princeton: Princeton University Press, 2020.

Bandura, Albert. "Moral Disengagement in the Perpetration of Inhumanities." *Personality and Social Psychology Review* 3, no. 3 (1999): 193–209.

Bates, Karen Grigsby. "A Different National Anthem, Before the Nation Was Ready for It." *Codeswitch*, November 2, 2017. https://www.npr.org/sections/codeswitch/2017/11/02/560948130/a-different-national-anthem-before-the-nation-was-ready-for-it.

Bateson, Mary Catherine. *Composing a Life*. New York: Grove Press, 1989.

Bell, Daniel A. *China's New Confucianism: Politics and Everyday Life in a Changing Society*. Princeton: Princeton University Press, 2008.

Billioud, Sébastien. "The Revival of Confucianism in the Sphere of Mores and the Reactivation of the Civil Religion Debate in China." In *Confucianism, a Habit of the Heart: Bellah, Civil Religion, and East Asia*, edited by P. J. Ivanhoe and Sungmoon Kim, 47–70. Albany: SUNY Press, 2016.

Callicott, J. Baird, and Roger T. Ames. *Nature in Asian Traditions of Thought: Essays in Environmental Philosophy*. Albany: SUNY Press, 1989.

Chan, Elton. *From Sage-Kings to Confucian Republic: The Political Theories of 'Jiaohua'*. Hong Kong: University of Hong Kong, 2014.

Chan, Elton. "Huang Zongxi as a Republican: A Theory of Governance for Confucian Democracy." *Dao: A Journal of Comparative Philosophy* 17 (2017): 203–218.

Chan, Joseph. "Democratic Equality or Confucian Hierarchy?" *Hierarchy and Equality Workshop sponsored by the Berggruen Institute* (2016).

Chan, Joseph 陳祖為. "天下無道，我們如何安身立命？ [If the Way Does Not Prevail, Where Shall We Take Our Stand?]." *StandNews*, June 2, 2020.

Chan, Sin Yee. "Gender Relationship Roles in the *Analects* and the *Mencius*." *Asian Philosophy* 2, no. 1 (2000): 115–132.

Chan, Sin Yee. "Would Confucianism Allow Two Men to Share a Peach? Compatibility Between Ancient Confucianism and Homosexuality." In *The Bloomsbury Research Handbook of Chinese Philosophy and Gender*, edited by Ann A. Pang-White, 173–201. London: Bloomsbury, 2016.

Chan, Wing-tsit. "Neo-Confucian Philosophical Poems." *Renditions* 4 (1975): 5–21.

Chan, Wing-tsit. "Chu Hsi and Quiet Sitting." In *Chu Hsi: New Studies*, 255–270. Honolulu: University of Hawaii, 1989.

Clague, Mark. "'This is America': Jimi Hendrix's Star Spangled Banner Journey as Psychedelic Citizenship." *Journal of the Society for American Music* 8, no. 4 (2014): 435–478.

Colby, Anne, and William Damon. *Some Do Care: Contemporary Lives of Moral Commitment*. New York: The Free Press, 1992.

Confucius. *The Analects of Confucius: A Philosophical Translation*. Translated by Roger T. Ames and Henry Rosemont Jr. New York: Ballantine Books, 1998.

Confucius. *The Original Analects: Sayings of Confucius and His Successors*. Translated by E. Bruce Brooks and A. Taeko Brooks. New York: Columbia University Press, 1998.

Confucius. *Analects, With Selections From Traditional Commentaries*. Translated by Edward Slingerland. Indianapolis: Hackett, 2003.

Confucius. *Understanding the Analects of Confucius: A New Translation of Lunyu With Annotations*. Translated by Peimin Ni. Albany: SUNY Press, 2017.

Cook, Scott B. "Unity and Diversity in the Musical Thought of Warring States China." PhD diss., University of Michigan Press, 1995.

Cook, Scott B. "*Yue Ji*—Record of Music: Introduction, Translation, Notes, and Commentary." *Asian Music* 26, no. 2 (1995): 1–95.

Cook, Scott B. "Musical Cultivation in the 'Xiu Wen' Chapter of the *Shuoyuan*." *Dao: A Journal of Comparative Philosophy* 16 (2017): 389–416.

Crawford, Matthew. *The World Beyond Your Head: Becoming an Individual in an Age of Distraction*. New York: Penguin, 2015.

Crockett, Zachary. "Are Gym Memberships Worth the Money?" *The Hustle*, January 5, 2019. https://thehustle.co/gym-membership-cost.

De Waal, Frans. *Mama's Last Hug: Animal Emotions and What They Tell Us About Ourselves*. New York: W. W. Norton & Co., 2019.

Delmas, Candice. *A Duty to Resist: When Disobedience Should be Uncivil*. New York: Oxford University Press, 2018.

Dimberg, Ronald G. *The Sage and Society: The Life and Thought of Ho Hsin-Yin*. Honolulu: University of Hawaii Press, 1974.

Feng, Youlan 冯友兰. 《三松堂全集》 [*Collected Works of Feng Youlan*]. Zhengzhou: Henan renmin chubanshe, 2001.

Flanagan, Owen. *Varieties of Moral Personality: Ethics and Psychological Realism*. Cambridge: Harvard University Press, 1991.

Flanagan, Owen. *The Geography of Morals: Varieties of Moral Possibility*. New York: Oxford University Press, 2017.

Flescher, Andrew M. *Heroes, Saints, & Ordinary Morality*. Washington, DC: Georgetown University Press, 2003.

Fuji, Michiaki 籐井倫明. 《朱熹思想結構探索》 [*Research on the Structure of Zhu Xi's Thought*]. Taipei: Taida chuban zhongxin, 2011.

Gardner, Daniel K. *Confucianism: A Very Short Introduction*. New York: Oxford University Press, 2014.

Giebel, Heidi M. *Ethical Excellence: Philosophers, Psychologists, and Real-Life Exemplars Show Us How to Achieve it*. Washington, DC: Catholic University of America Press, 2021.

Goldin, Paul R. *Confucianism*. Berkeley: University of California Press, 2011.

Goldin, Paul R. "Reception of the *Odes* in the Warring States Era." In *After Confucius: Studies in Early Chinese Philosophy*, 19–35. Honolulu: University of Hawaii, 2005.

Gosetti-Ferencei, Jennifer. *On Being and Becoming: An Existentialist Approach to Life*. New York: Oxford University Press, 2020.

Greene, Melissa Fay. "30 Years Ago, Romania Deprived Thousands of Babies of Human Contact." *The Atlantic* July/August (2020). https://www.theatlantic.com/magazine/archive/2020/07/can-an-unloved-child-learn-to-love/612253/.

Gross, Rita M. *Buddhism After Patriarchy: A Feminist History, Analysis, and Reconstruction of Buddhism*. Albany: SUNY Press, 1992.

Hadot, Pierre. *Philosophy as a Way of Life: Spiritual Exercises From Socrates to Foucault*. Cambridge, MA: Blackwell, 1995.

Hallie, Philip. *Lest Innocent Blood be Shed: The Story of the Village of Le Chambon and How Goodness Happened There*. New York: Harper and Row, 1979.

Harold, James. "On the Ancient Idea That Music Shapes Character." *Dao: A Journal of Comparative Philosophy* 15 (2016): 341–354.

Higgins, Kathleen. "Confucius' Opposition to the 'New Music.'" *Dao: A Journal of Comparative Philosophy* 16 (2017): 309–323.

Hourdequin, Marion. "Engagement, Withdrawal, and Social Reform: Confucian and Contemporary Perspectives." *Philosophy East & West* 60, no. 3 (2010): 369–390.

Huang, Yushun. *Voice from the East: The Chinese Theory of Justice*. Translated by Pingping and Wang Hou Keyou. Reading: Paths International Ltd., 2016.

Huang, Zongxi. *Waiting for the Dawn*. Translated by William Theodore DeBary. New York: Columbia University Press, 1993.

Huff, Benjamin. "Servants of Heaven: The Place of Virtue in the Confucian Cosmos." *International Communication of Chinese Culture* 4, no. 2 (2017): 271–298.

Ing, Michael. *The Vulnerability of Integrity in Early Confucian Thought.* Oxford: Oxford University Press, 2017.

Israel, George L. *Doing Good and Ridding Evil in Ming China: The Political Career of Wang Yangming.* Leiden and Boston: Brill, 2014.

Ivanhoe, Philip J. *Confucian Moral Self Cultivation.* 2nd ed. Indianapolis/Cambridge: Hackett, 2000.

Ivanhoe, Philip J. "Filial Piety as a Virtue." In *Working Virtue: Virtue Ethics and Contemporary Moral Problems,* edited by Rebecca Walker, and Philip J. Ivanhoe, 297–312. Oxford: Oxford University Press, 2007.

Ivanhoe, Philip J. *Confucian Reflections: Ancient Wisdom for Modern Times.* New York: Routledge, 2013.

Ivanhoe, Philip J. *Oneness: East Asian Conceptions of Virtue, Happiness, and How We Are All Connected.* New York: Oxford University Press, 2017.

Ivanhoe, Philip J. "Death and Dying in the Analects." In *Mortality in Chinese Thought,* edited by Amy Olberding and P. J. Ivanhoe, 136–152. Albany: SUNY Press, 2011.

Ivanhoe, Philip J., Owen Flanagan, Victoria S. Harrison, Hagop Sarkissian, and Eric Schwitzgebel. *The Oneness Hypothesis: Beyond the Boundary of the Self.* New York: Columbia University Press, 2018.

Jiang, Qing. *A Confucian Constitutional Order: How China's Ancient Past Can Shape Its Political Future.* Translated by Edmund Ryden. Princeton: Princeton University Press, 2013.

Jiang, Qing. "Only Confucians Can Make a Place for Modern Women." In *Voices from the Chinese Century: Public Intellectual Debate from Contemporary China,* edited by Timothy Cheek, David Ownby, and Joshua A. Fogel, 318–342. New York: Columbia University Press, 2019.

Kalton, Michael, ed. *The Four-Seven Debate: An Annotated Translation of the Most Famous Controversy in Korean Neo-Confucian Thought.* Albany: SUNY Press, 1994.

Kim, Sungmoon. "The Virtue of Incivility: Confucian Communitarianism Beyond Docility." *Philosophy and Social Criticism* 37, no. 1 (2011): 25–48.

Lee, Pauline C. "Li Zhi and John Stuart Mill: A Confucian Feminist Critique of Liberal Feminism." In *The Sage and the Second Sex: Confucianism, Ethics, and Gender*, edited by Chenyang Li, 113–132. Chicago: Open Court, 2000.

Liu, JeeLoo. *Neo-Confucianism: Metaphysics, Mind, and Morality*. New York: Wiley-Blackwell, 2017.

Mabuchi, Masaya. "'Quiet Sitting' in Neo-Confucianism." In *Asian Traditions of Meditation*, edited by Halvor Eifring, 207–226. Honolulu: University of Hawaii, 2016.

MacIntyre, Alasdair C. *Whose Justice? Which Rationality?* Notre Dame: University of Notre Dame Press, 1988.

MacIntyre, Alasdair C. *Three Rival Versions of Moral Enquiry: Encyclopedia, Genealogy, and Tradition: Being Gifford Lectures Delivered in the University of Edinburgh in 1988*. Notre Dame, IN: University of Notre Dame Press, 1990.

Mencius. *Mencius*. Translated by D. C. Lau. London: Penguin, 1970.

Mengzi. *Mengzi: With Selections from Traditional Commentaries*. Translated by Bryan Van Norden. Indianapolis: Hackett, 2008.

Mower, Deborah. "Situationism and Confucian Virtue Ethics." *Ethical Theory and Moral Practice* 16 (2013): 113–137.

Munro, Donald. *The Concept of Man in Ancient China*. Stanford: Stanford University Press, 1969.

Munro, Donald. *A Chinese Ethics for the New Century: The Ch'ien Mu Lectures in History and Culture, and Other Essays on Science and Confucian Ethics*. Hong Kong: The Chinese University Press, 2005.

Murdoch, Iris. "On 'God' and 'Good'." In *The Sovereignty of the Good*, 46–76. New York: Routledge, 1970.

Murdoch, Iris. "The Sovereignty of the Good Over Other Concepts." In *The Sovereignty of the Good*, 77–104. New York: Routledge, 1970.

Murray, Charles Shaar. *Crosstown Traffic: Jimi Hendrix and the Post-War Rock 'n' Roll Revolution*. New York: St. Martin's, 1989.

Narvaez, Darcia, and Daniel K. Lapsely. "The Psychological Foundations of Everyday Morality and Moral Expertise." In *Moral Psychology at the Crossroads*, edited by Daniel K. Lapsley and F. Clark Power, 140–165. Notre Dame, IN: University of Notre Dame Press, 2005.

Narvaez, Darcia, Daniel K. Lapsely, Scott Hagele, and Benjamin Lasky. "Moral Chronicity and Social Information Processing: Tests of a Social Cognitive Approach to the Moral Personality." *Journal of Research in Personality* 40 (2006): 966–985.

Neville, Robert Cummings. *Boston Confucianism: Portable Tradition in the Late-Modern World*. Albany: SUNY Press, 2000.

Neville, Robert Cummings. *The Good is One, Its Manifestations Many: Confucian Essays on Metaphysics, Morals, Rituals, Institutions, and Genders*. Albany: SUNY Press, 2016.

Nussbaum, Martha. *Love's Knowledge: Essays on Philosophy and Literature*. New York: Oxford University Press, 1990.

Nussbaum, Martha. "Perception and Revolution: *The Princess Casamassima* and the Political Imagination." In *Love's Knowledge: Essays on Philosophy and Literature*. New York: Oxford University Press, 1990.

Nussbaum, Martha. "Undemocratic Vistas." In *Philosophical Interventions: Reviews 1986–2011*, New York: Oxford University Press, 2012.

Nussbaum, Martha, and Amartya Sen. "Internal Criticism and the Indian Rationalist Tradition." In *Relativism: Interpretation and Confrontation*, edited by Michael Krausz, 299–325. Notre Dame: University of Notre Dame Press, 1989.

Olberding, Amy. "Slowing Death Down: Mourning in the Analects." In *Confucius Now: Contemporary Encounters With the* Analects, edited by David Jones, 137–149. La Salle: Open Court, 2008.

Olberding, Amy. "'Ascending the Hall': Style and Moral Improvement in the *Analects*." *Philosophy East & West* 59, no. 4 (2009): 503–522.

Olberding, Amy. "I Know Not "Seems": Grief for Parents in the *Analects*." In *Mortality in Chinese Thought*, edited by Amy Olberding and P. J. Ivanhoe, 153–176. Albany: SUNY Press, 2011.

Olberding, Amy. "Other People Die and *That* Is the Problem." In *The Bloomsbury Research Handbook of Early Chinese Ethics and Political Philosophy*, edited by Alexus McLeod, 205–224. London: Bloomsbury, 2019.

Olberding, Amy. *The Wrong of Rudeness: Learning Modern Civility From Ancient Chinese Philosophy*. New York: Oxford University Press, 2019.

Olberding, Amy, and P. J. Ivanhoe, eds. *Mortality in Chinese Thought* Albany: SUNY Press, 2011.

Pang-White, Ann A. *The Confucian Four Books for Women: A New Translation of the Nü Sishu and the Commentary of Wang Xiang*. New York: Oxford University Press, 2018.

Parker, Ian. "The Gift." *The New Yorker* August 2 (2004): 54.

Parks Daloz, Laurent A., Cheryl H. Keen, James P. Keen, and Sharon Daloz Parks. *Common Fire: Leading Lives of Commitment in a Complex World*. Boston: Beacon Press, 1996.

Peng, Guoxiang. "Death as the Ultimate Concern in Neo-Confucian Tradition: Wang Yangming's Followers as an Example." In *Mortality in Chinese Thought*, edited by Amy Olberding and P. J. Ivanhoe, 271–295. Albany: SUNY Press, 2011.

Peng, Guoxiang 彭国翔. "儒学复兴的深思 [Reflections on the Revival of Confucianism]." 《二十一世纪经济报道》 [*21st Century Economic Report*], 34–35, December 18, 2006.

Plato. *Complete Works*. Indianapolis: Hackett, 1997.

Prebish, Charles. *Buddhism—the American Experience*. Journal of Buddhist Ethics Online Books, Inc., 2003.

Putilin, Dimitri. "Tribalism and Universalism: Reflections and Scientific Evidence." In *The Oneness Hypothesis: Beyond the Boundary of the Self*, edited by Philip J. Ivanhoe, Owen Flanagan, Victoria S. Harrison, Hagop Sarkissian, and Eric Schwitzgebel, 351–370. New York: Columbia University Press, 2018.

Raphals, Lisa. *Sharing the Light: Representations of Women and Virtue in Early China*. Albany: SUNY Press, 1998.

Roos, Meghan. "January 12: The Date Most New Year's Resolutions Will Slip." *Women's Running*, January 12, 2018. https://www.womensrunning.com/culture/january-12-date-likely-kick-new-years-resolutions/.

Rorty, Richard. "Human Rights, Rationality, and Sentimentality." In *On Human Rights: The Oxford Amnesty Lectures, 1993*, edited by Stephen Shute and Susan Hurley, 167–185, New York: Basic Books, 1993.

Rosemont Jr., Henry, and Roger T. Ames. *The Chinese Classic of Family Reverence": A Philosophical Translation of the* Xiaojing. Honolulu: University of Hawaii Press, 2009.

Rosenlee, Li-Hsiang Lisa. *Confucianism and Women: A Philosophical Interpretation*. Albany: SUNY Press, 2006.

Roth, Michael S. *Safe Enough Spaces: A Pragmatist's Approach to Inclusion, Free Speech, and Political Correctness on College Campuses*. New Haven: Yale University Press, 2019.

Rothman, Joshua. "A New Theory of Distraction." *The New Yorker*, June 16, 2015.

Sarkissian, Hagop. "Minor Tweaks, Major Payoffs: The Problems and Promise of Situationism in Moral Philosophy." *Philosopher's Imprint* 10, no. 9 (2010): 1–15.

Sarkissian, Hagop. "Recent Approaches to Confucian Filial Morality." *Philosophy Compass* 5, no. 9 (2010): 725–734.

Sartwell, Crispin. "Confucius and Country Music." *Philosophy East & West* 43, no. 2 (1993): 243–254.

Seligman, Adam B., Robert P. Weller, Michael J. Puett, and Bennett Simon. *Ritual and Its Consequences: An Essay in the Limits of Sincerity*. New York: Oxford University Press, 2008.

Shils, Edward. *Tradition*. Chicago: University of Chicago Press, 1981.

Slingerland, Edward. "The Situationist Critique and Early Confucian Virtue Ethics." *Ethics* 121, no. 2 (2011): 390–419.

Slingerland, Edward. *Trying Not to Try: The Art and Science of Spontaneity*. New York: Crown, 2014.

Slote, Michael. *Moral Sentimentalism*. New York: Oxford University Press, 2010.

Stalnaker, Aaron. *Overcoming Our Evil: Human Nature and Spiritual Exercises in Xunzi and Augustine*. Washington, DC: Georgetown University Press, 2006.

Stalnaker, Aaron. *Mastery, Dependence, and the Ethics of Authority*. New York: Oxford University Press, 2020.

Stephens, Thomas B. *Order and Discipline in China: The Shanghai Mixed Court 1911–27*. Seattle: University of Washington Press, 1992.

Stohr, Karen E. "Moral Cacophony: When Continence Is a Virtue." *The Journal of Ethics* 7 (2003): 339–363.

Sun, Anna. *Confucianism as a World Religion: Contested Histories and Contemporary Realities*. Princeton: Princeton University Press, 2013.

Swain, Tony. *Confucianism in China: An Introduction*. New York: Bloomsbury, 2017.

Swanton, Christine. *Virtue Ethics: A Pluralistic View*. Oxford: Oxford University Press, 2003.

Tan, Sor-hoon. *Confucian Democracy: A Deweyan Reconstruction*. Albany: SUNY Press, 2004.

Tan, Sor-hoon. "Authoritative Master Kong (Confucius) in an Authoritarian Age." *Dao: A Journal of Comparative Philosophy* 9, no. 2 (2010): 137–149.

Tang, Zhonggang 汤忠钢. 《德性与政治：牟宗三新儒家政治哲学研究》 [*Virtue and Politics: Research on Mou Zongsan's New Confucian Political Philosophy*]. Beijing: Zhongguo Yanshi chubanshe, 2008.

Tatum, Becky L. "The Link Between Rap Music and Youth Crime and Violence: A Review of the Literature and Issues for Future Research." *The Justice Professional* 11, no. 3 (1999): 339–353.

Tavor, Ori. "Embodying the Dead: Ritual as Preventative Therapy in Chinese Ancestor Worship and Funerary Practices." *Journal of Ritual Studies* 34, no. 1 (2020): 31–42.

Tessman, Lisa. *Burdened Virtues: Virtue Ethics for Liberatory Struggles*. Oxford: Oxford University Press, 2005.

"The Origin of New Year's Resolutions." *The Economist*, January 5, 2018.

Tiwald, Justin. "Zhu Xi on Self-Focused Vs. Other-Focused Empathy." In *Dao Companion to Zhu Xi's Philosophy*, edited by Kai-chiu Ng and Yong Huang, 963–980. Dordrecht: Springer, 2020.

Tu, Wei-ming. "The Continuity of Being: Chinese Visions of Nature." In *Nature in Asian Traditions of Thought: Essays in Environmental Philosophy*, edited by J. Baird Callicott and Roger T. Ames, 67–78. Albany: SUNY Press, 1989.

Tu, Wei-ming, and Mary Evelyn Tucker, eds. *Confucian Spirituality, Volume One*. New York: Crossroad Publishing Co., 2003.

Tu, Wei-ming, and Mary Evelyn Tucker, eds. *Confucian Spirituality, Volume Two*. New York: Crossroad Publishing Co., 2004.

Tucker, John A. "Skepticism and the Neo-Confucian Canon: Itō Jinsai's Philosophical Critique of the *Great Learning*." *Dao: A Journal of Comparative Philosophy* 12 (2013): 11–39.

Van Norden, Bryan W. *Virtue Ethics and Consequentialism in Early Chinese Philosophy*. New York: Cambridge University Press, 2007.

Van Norden, Bryan W., and Justin Tiwald. *Readings in Later Chinese Philosophy*. Cambridge: Hackett, 2014.

Van Oosten, Johanna M. F., Jochen Peter, and Patti M. Valkenburg. "The Influence of Sexual Music Videos on Adolescents' Misogynistic Beliefs: The Role of Video Content, Gender, and Affective Engagement." *Communication Research* 42, no. 7 (2015): 986–1008.

Wang, Yangming. *Instructions for Practical Living*. Translated by Wing-tsit Chan. New York: Columbia University Press, 1963.

Wang, Yangming. *The Philosophical Letters of Wang Yang-Ming*. Translated by Julia Ching. Canberra: Australia National University Press, 1972.

Waxman, Olivia B. "Trying to Get in Shape in 2020? Here's the History Behind the Common New Year's Resolution." *Time*, January 8, 2020.

Weber, Max. "Science as a Vocation." *Daedalus* 87, no. 1 (1958): 111–134.

Wolf, Susan. "Moral Saints." *Journal of Philosophy* 79, no. 8 (1982): 419–439.

Woodruff, Paul. *Reverence: Renewing a Forgotten Virtue*. Oxford: Oxford University Press, 2001.

Wu, Pei-yi. *The Confucian's Progress: Autobiographical Writings in Traditional China*. Princeton, NJ: Princeton University Press, 1990.

Wu, Yubi. *The Journal of Wu Yubi: The Path to Sagehood*. Translated by Theresa Kelleher. Indianapolis: Hackett, 2013.

Xu, Fuguan 徐復觀. 《中國人性論史》 [*History of Chinese Human Nature*]. Taipei: Taiwan Shangwu Yinshuguan, 1969.

Xunzi. *Xunzi: The Complete Text*. Translated by Eric L. Hutton. Princeton: Princeton University Press, 2014.

Yang, Fenggang. "Confucianism as Civil Religion." In *Confucianism, a Habit of the Heart: Bellah, Civil Religion, and East Asia*, edited by P. J. Ivanhoe and Sungmoon Kim, 25–46. Albany: SUNY Press, 2016.

Yang, Fenggang 杨凤岗. "对于儒教之为教的社会学思考 [Sociological Reflections on the Religiosity of Confucianism]." *Journal of Lanzhou University (Social Sciences)* 36, no. 3 (2008).

Yao, Xinzhong. *An Introduction to Confucianism*. Cambridge: Cambridge University Press, 2000.

Yu, Dan. *Confucius From the Heart: Ancient Wisdom for Today's World*. New York: Atria Books, 2010.

Yearley, Lee H. "Freud and China: The Pursuit of the Self and Other Fugitive Notions." In *The Reception and Rendition of Freud in China: China's Freudian Slip*, edited by Tao Jiang and Philip J. Ivanhoe, 169–195. New York: Routledge, 2013.

Yu, Jiyuan. *The Ethics of Confucius and Aristotle: Mirrors of Virtue*. New York: Routledge, 2007.

Zhang, Xianglong 张祥龙. "成立儒家文化特区或保护区的理由与方式 [Reasons and Methods for Creating Confucian Special Cultural Zones or Protection Zones]." 《儒家网》 [*Confucian Web*] (2015). https://www.rujiazg.com/article/5376.

Zhang, Xianglong 张祥龙. 《家与孝：从中西间视野看》 [*Family and Filial Piety: As Viewed From Between China and the West*]. Beijing: Sanlian Shudian, 2017.

Zhu, Xi. *Learning to be a Sage*. Translated by Daniel K. Gardner. Berkeley: University of California Press, 1990.

Zhu, Xi. *Further Reflections on Things At Hand*. Translated by Allan Wittenborn. Lanham: University Press of America, 1991.

Zhu, Xi, and Zuqian Lu. *Reflections on Things At Hand*. Translated by Wing-tsit Chan. New York: Columbia University Press, 1967.

Zhu, Xi 朱熹. 《朱子全書》 [*Complete Works of Master Zhu*]. Shanghai and Hefei: Shanghai Guji chubanshe and Anhui Jiaoyu chubanshe, 2002.

Zhu, Xi. *Zhu Xi: Selected Writings*. Translated by Philip J. Ivanhoe et al. New York: Oxford University Press, 2019.

INDEX